Praise for *Real-Time Marketing & PR*

"With his acute ear for the cash register and his journalist's sense of urgency, no one understands the value of time better than David Meerman Scott. He teaches marketers and C-level execs how to use time and urgency to gain huge competitive advantage. Read *Real-Time Marketing & PR*. Make money while your competitors sleep."

—**Brian Fetherstonhaugh**
Chairman & CEO, OgilvyOne Worldwide

"If you are not hooked (hook, line, and sinker) within 10 minutes of starting David Meerman Scott's wonderful new book, well, I fear for you. Beautifully written, cases that reach out from the page and grab you and shake you, and practical advice that anyone, anywhere can use in a flash to make hay. I simply loved this book, and doubled my knowledge along the way."

—**Tom Peters**
Author of *The Little Big Things*

"Information is like running water. The speed of information as it cascades through digital channels has been dramatically accelerated and amplified requiring marketing to change in order to catch up to this new reality. *Real-Time* is the keyword."

—**Hiroshi Ishii**
Muriel R. Cooper Professor of Media Arts and Sciences,
Massachusetts Institute of Technology,
and Associate Director of MIT Media Laboratory

"Right now, opportunities are passing you by as prospective customers and journalists search and chat online for solutions to their problems. David's new book, *Real-Time Marketing & PR*, gives you the playbook and toolbox to help you act fast and be present as these conversations emerge. However, the real message of the book is one of mind-set: How can you deliver value faster today? Entrepreneurs and intrapreneurs focused on growing their profits, customers, and influence *now* can't afford to wait to read this book."

—**Richard Jackson**
Chairman & CEO, Jackson Healthcare

"We all know that opportunities and threats from the digital world often arrive without warning. They can't wait for discussion at monthly planning meetings. Hell, most times they can't wait for you to finish lunch! David Meerman Scott's book provides a rationale to help you create real-time mind-set in your own organization."

—**Bill Sledzik, Associate Professor**
School of Journalism & Mass Communication, Kent State University

"The world has changed dramatically, and we have now entered a new, real-time era. Dusty business plans are now being crushed by right-now strategy and adaptation. David's book offers the new road map to entrepreneurs, business leaders, and individuals. It's made a big impact on the way I approach our business and our customers; the insight I've gained by reading it is priceless. This important and thoughtful book is a must-read to compete in the next era of business, and life."

—**Josh Linkner**
Chairman/Founder, ePrize
and author of *Disciplined Dreaming:
A Proven System to Unleash Business Creativity*

Also by David Meerman Scott

The New Rules of Marketing and PR (Second Edition): *How to Use Social Media, Blogs, News Releases, Online Video, and Viral Marketing to Reach Buyers Directly*

Marketing Lessons from the Grateful Dead: *What Every Business Can Learn from the Most Iconic Band in History* (with Brian Halligan)

World Wide Rave: *Creating Triggers that Get Millions of People to Spread Your Ideas and Share Your Stories*

Tuned In: *Uncover the Extraordinary Opportunities that Lead to Business Breakthroughs* (with Craig Stull and Phil Myers)

Cashing in with Content: *How Innovative Marketers Use Digital Information to Turn Browsers into Buyers*

Eyeball Wars: *A Novel of Dot-Com Intrigue*

REAL-TIME
MARKETING & PR

HOW TO INSTANTLY ENGAGE YOUR MARKET, CONNECT WITH CUSTOMERS, AND CREATE PRODUCTS THAT GROW YOUR BUSINESS NOW

DAVID MEERMAN SCOTT

WILEY

John Wiley & Sons, Inc.

Published by John Wiley & Sons, Inc., Hoboken, New Jersey.
Published simultaneously in Canada.

For general information on our other products and services or for technical support,
please contact our Customer Care Department within the United States at (800) 762-2974,
outside the United States at (317) 572-3993 or fax (317) 572-4002.

Wiley also publishes its books in a variety of electronic formats. Some content that appears
in print may not be available in electronic books. For more information about Wiley products, visit our web site at www.wiley.com.

ISBN 978-0-470-64595-6 (cloth); ISBN 978-0-470-93017-5 (ebk); ISBN 978-0-470-
93023-6 (ebk); ISBN 978-0-470-93024-3

Printed in the United States of America

10 9 8 7 6 5 4 3 2 1

Contents

Prologue

*A*wareness *of information as it happens, in real time, can give you an enormous competitive advantage—if you know how to use it. This was a key lesson I learned working on Wall Street in the go-go 1980s.*

It's 1985, and I'm on the institutional trading floor of an investment bank in lower Manhattan. It's nearly noon, time for lunch, and nothing has happened all morning. But none of the bond traders leaves. They're scared they might miss something. The bank doesn't want them leaving either, so everyone gets pizza delivered to their desks.

Inhabiting a world of split-second decisions, bond traders earn big money making trades involving hundreds of millions of dollars. It's a daily battle that involves incredibly long periods of tedium punctuated by occasional short bursts of intense action.

Fortunes are made in seconds; reputations lost in a minute.

Nothing is happening now, though. All is quiet, and boredom reigns because no significant news has broken all morning.

Some traders desperately search their real-time news feeds from Dow Jones, Reuters, and the Associated Press for an angle, any angle, in the quiet market. What's Ronald Reagan up to today? What about Margaret Thatcher? Any news from Paul Volcker, the Federal Reserve chairman? Any economic data due to be released this afternoon? Any large companies announcing quarterly earnings today?

As they pore through data and news, the traders are poised, ready to commit huge sums of money when the moment is right. They peer intently at the Bloomberg screens displaying bond prices *the moment they change*. Data from futures markets and stock exchanges update *the instant a trade is made*.

Speed on the trading floor is so crucial that traders are linked one to one with their counterparts at other institutions by direct, dedicated lines—just like the Kremlin and the White House.

At a nearby desk, I see a phone panel light up (no ringing on the trading floor), and a trader answers by jabbing the button with his middle finger. But when he sits back relaxed, his body language tells me he's simply swapping the latest off-color joke or talking football.

Suddenly, one of the senior traders yells, loud as he can: "The Fed's in!"

For a split second, the room is completely silent as all listen.

When the senior trader then bellows "Buying treasuries!" it's as if a bomb has hit. The entire room erupts in highly organized chaos. Pizza is tossed aside, and phones are grabbed in one fluid movement. It's time to earn those huge salaries.

In a heartbeat, everyone is on at least one phone, and many are on two or more, alerting customers in an instant: "The Fed is in!"

Within seconds, the screens light up in seas of green as bond prices rise steeply across the board. Before the same minute expires, financial newswires like Dow Jones and Reuters write and issue "newsflashes" that appear instantly on trading room screens from Albuquerque to Zagreb. *Within just 60 seconds, everywhere knows and everyone is equal again.* The competitive advantage disappears.

But within that minute the traders who got their orders placed a split-second faster had earned their daily bread. *Being first* with the news is valuable currency that earns them lucrative deals from their clients. Hearing it first and acting on it fast equals money—*lots of money*—on Wall Street.

Since I first witnessed a Wall Street minute in 1985, trading technology has advanced light-years. But what I saw then was still new: Technology was transforming financial trading into a game where instant information informs split-second decisions worth millions of dollars.

It's impossible to overstate the impact of innovations in computing and telecommunications on the financial markets in the 1980s. Within a decade finance was transformed from a clubby, old-boys' network to a 24-hour global trading system. With that revolutionary shift a new currency of success emerged: the ability to gather, interpret, and react to new information in fractions of a second—real time.

It has taken a quarter century. But in fields like marketing and public relations the impact of the real-time revolution in finance is finally beginning to hit the so-called "real economy."

Who's leading the way? As you will read in these pages, it's not mega-corporations with billion-dollar information technology (IT) budgets. Far from it!

In today's real-time revolution the swift are out in front. As you discover in Chapter 1, one of the largest, most technically sophisticated marketers in the United States proved no match for one irate Canadian with a broken guitar and a video camera.

Revolution Time

Wake Up, It's Revolution Time!

Your accustomed methods and processes may be already fatally out of sync with the world around you. The narrative of your business now unfolds, minute by minute, in real time. And it's driven by your customers, talking among themselves—no longer guided by the mass media your ad budget can buy.

In a world where speed and agility are now essential to success, most organizations still operate slowly and deliberately, cementing each step months in advance, responding to new developments with careful but time-consuming processes.

This time lag can leave your business fatally exposed. But it doesn't have to! As you discover in Part One of *Real-Time Marketing & PR*, there are clear paths to follow in adapting your course and your culture to the new environment.

Allow me to introduce you to the rules of real-time marketing and public relations (PR).

1

Grow Your Business Now

In the emerging real-time business environment, where public discourse is no longer dictated by the mass media, size is no longer a decisive advantage. Speed and agility win.

In this chapter we examine a "Dave versus Goliath" contest that shows how even one individual can outgun one of the largest, most "scientific" marketing, PR, and customer-service organizations on the planet. We also discover how other agile players quickly harness the momentum of Dave's slingshot.

> Now, more than at any other time in history, speed and agility are decisive competitive advantages.

"My God, they're throwing guitars out there," said a woman in a window seat as passengers on a United Airlines flight waited to deplane in Chicago on March 31, 2008.

Singer-songwriter Dave Carroll and fellow members of Sons of Maxwell, a Canadian pop-folk band, knew instantly *whose* guitars. Flying from home in Halifax, Nova Scotia, for a one-week tour of Nebraska, their four guitars were in the airplane's hold. Sure enough, when the bass player looked out the window he witnessed United baggage handlers tossing his bass.

The band did not have to wait to retrieve their luggage in Omaha, their final destination, to start complaining, because they had actually observed this abuse of their equipment. As they made their way out of the plane, they told the flight attendants what they had seen. "Talk to the ground staff," they were told. But the O'Hare ground staff said, "Talk to the ground staff in Omaha."

Sure enough, when Dave opened his hard-shell case in Omaha he discovered his $3,500 Taylor guitar had been smashed. And United Airlines staff in Omaha refused to accept his claim.

So Dave spent months phoning and emailing United in pursuit of $1,200 to cover the cost of repairs. At each step, United staff refused to accept responsibility and shuffled him off: from telephone reps in India, to the central baggage office in New York, to the Chicago baggage office.

Finally, after nine futile months, Dave got a flat "no." No, he was told, he would not receive any form of compensation from United.

"At that moment, it occurred to me I'd been fighting a losing battle all this time," Dave told me. "I got sucked into their cycle of insanity. I called and emailed and jumped through hoops, just as they told me to do. The system is designed to frustrate customers into giving up their claims, and United is very good at it. However, I realized that, as a musician, I wasn't without options. So when I finally got the 'no,' I said, 'I urge you to reconsider, because I'm a singer-songwriter and I'm going to write three songs about United Airlines and post them on YouTube.'"

Making good on this promise, on July 6, 2009, Dave posted on YouTube "United Breaks Guitars," a catchy tune with memorable lyrics that tells the saga of his broken guitar:

> United, United, you broke my Taylor Guitar
> United, United, some big help you are
> You broke it, you should fix it
> You're liable, just admit it
> I should have flown with someone else
> Or gone by car
> 'Cause United breaks guitars
> Yeah, United breaks guitars

Within just four days, the video reached 1 million views on YouTube. And then another million. And another.

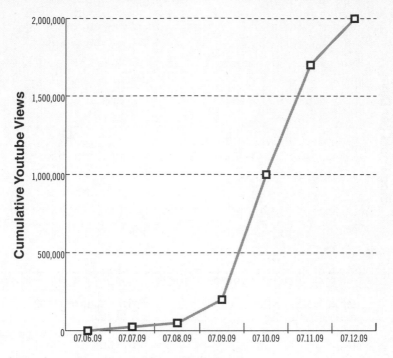

United Breaks Guitars: YouTube Video Views

Momentum built from July 8 to 11 as up to 100 bloggers a day alerted their readers to the video. Incidentally, notice how the number of blog posts per day follows a bell-shaped curve—starting slowly (because Dave Carroll wasn't well known), building to a peak, then trailing off. We come back to this in Chapter 3 when I discuss the importance of what I call the Real-Time Law of Normal Distribution.

This is a story about speed in media relations.

"United Breaks Guitars" soon became a real-time phenomenon that propelled Dave into the spotlight. It continued to grow in the spotlight because Dave was ready and able to speak with the media in real time, conducting dozens of interviews in a few days while the story was hot.

This is also a story about real-time market engagement.

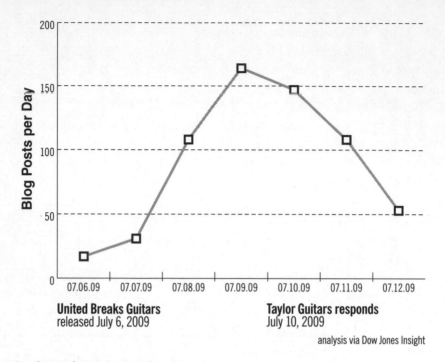

United Breaks Guitars
released July 6, 2009

Taylor Guitars responds
July 10, 2009

analysis via Dow Jones Insight

United Breaks Guitars: Blog Posts per Day

The maker of Dave's instrument, Taylor Guitars, seized the real-time op-portunity to build goodwill among customers. Within days of Dave's initial YouTube post, Bob Taylor, the company's president, had his own video up on YouTube, advising traveling musicians how to pack equipment and use airline rules to best advantage.

There's more: This is a story of real-time product creation, too.

Calton Cases, a specialist maker of highly durable instrument cases for professional musicians, likewise seized the moment. Within mere days, Cal-ton had a new product on the market: the Dave Carroll Traveler's Edition Guitar Case.

Finally, this is about a company that chose not to connect with customers.

As millions of potential customers saw a video that persuasively cast its brand in the worst possible light, negating the value of tens of millions of dollars in media advertising, United Airlines chose to make absolutely no response. This from the largest player in one of the most consumer-facing of industries, an industry that over decades has spent billions on advertising, public relations, and "scientific" customer-service methodology.

As a YouTube phenomenon "United Breaks Guitars" has drawn attention from thousands of media commentators. But two aspects have been overlooked: the reasons why Dave's video gained so much momentum, and the way agile players on the periphery were able to surf that momentum.

Dave's Slingshot Goes Viral on Goliath

I learned about "United Breaks Guitars" from one of my readers three days after Dave posted it on YouTube. At that time the video had about 200,000 views, and after watching for 30 seconds I said, "I need to blog this *right now!*" It was so fresh and exciting that I wanted my blog readers and Twitter followers to hear about it from me first.

So I quickly wrote a blog post, embedded the video, and pushed it live within half an hour of discovering it. I also tweeted the link to my 20,000 (at that time) Twitter followers. I was just one of many triggers that helped spread the video to millions. But I was early—because I reacted *in real time*.

The video's first viewing growth spike came on Day 2 (July 7). After *The Consumerist* web site posted a link to it, the number of views jumped to 25,000. The *Los Angeles Times* called Dave that day. So did several local Canadian publications.

Next day, July 8, after CNN broadcast part of "United Breaks Guitars," Dave was suddenly the media celebrity of the moment.

Improvising with the snowball, Dave mounted a real-time PR effort that many agencies would be hard-pressed to match. Family members set up a communication room, fielding media requests that flooded in by phone and email, and triaging Dave's schedule in real time to ensure he made it onto the highest-profile outlets. His 15 minutes of fame were happening *right now*, and he needed to ride it as hard as he could.

"I knew I was reaching a big audience when I was about to tape an interview with CTV and the host said I was on *The Situation Room with Wolf Blitzer* on CNN at that moment," Dave says. "We raced from one interview to

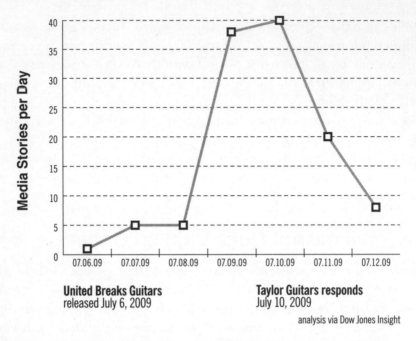

United Breaks Guitars: Mainstream Media Stories per Day (television, radio, newspaper, magazines)

another. While someone drove me studio to studio, I did newspaper interviews on my cell phone."

In this way, Dave managed to do dozens of interviews in a few days with print outlets like the *Wall Street Journal, USA Today*, and the *Los Angeles Times* and broadcasters like CBS, CNN, and FOX. With each media appearance the number of YouTube views spiked higher.

Evolution of a Real-Time Media Explosion

Monday, July 6, 2009: Dave Carroll posts "United Breaks Guitars" at midnight Atlantic Daylight Time. "There were six views by the time I went to bed," he says.

July 7, 8:00 A.M.: "There were 330 views when I woke up," Dave says. "I was excited, and called the videographer." That morning,

Carroll is interviewed by his local newspaper, the *Halifax Herald*, and an online story appeared later in the day.

July 7, 12:00 P.M.: Video up to 5,000 views. *The Consumerist* web site posts a link to the video that delivers 25,000 YouTube views in a few hours. Bob Taylor of Taylor Guitars and Jim Laffoley of Calton Cases also see the video. Laffoley contacts Carroll, asking how they might collaborate. *Got that? A mere 12 hours after posting the video, Carroll had an offer to collaborate with Calton Cases!*

July 7, 8:00 P.M.: While Dave Carroll is playing a gig, United Airlines calls and leaves a message: They want to speak with him. So does the *Los Angeles Times*.

July 8: "By Wednesday, things got busy," Carroll says. He is interviewed by the *LA Times* and several Canadian publications. Parts of the video air on CNN, as the video passes 50,000 views on YouTube. FOX News and CBS both call for interviews. United calls again, and Carroll sets a time to talk—two days later. *Why bother rushing to talk with United? After all, they blew him off for nine months.*

July 9: As the video passes 200,000 YouTube views one of my readers points me to it and I post it to my blog right away. Laffoley and Dave make plans for the Calton Cases Dave Carroll Traveler's Edition Guitar Case.

July 10: "United Breaks Guitars" reaches 1 million YouTube views. Taylor Guitars posts its YouTube response. Dave talks to United Airlines by phone—and even now they don't apologize. But with some weasel words about the "regrettable incident," he is finally offered compensation. He rejects this as too late, suggesting the money be given to someone in a similar situation.

July 12: "United Breaks Guitars" reaches 2 million YouTube views.

July 19: Web site for Calton Cases Dave Carroll Traveler's Edition Guitar Case goes live. *Note how quickly the new product is developed and launched.*

July 22: BBC television interviews Dave. "Minutes after the interview ran, competing stations called wanting to speak with me. I did nine phone interviews in one day," Carroll says. "United Breaks Guitars" is released on iTunes and becomes the number one country and Western download in the United Kingdom.

(continued)

> (*continued*)
>
> **July 23:** "United Breaks Guitars" reaches 3 million YouTube views.
>
> **August 18:** The second song in Dave's United trilogy is released.
>
> **September 14:** In a meeting at O'Hare Airport (scene of the crime, so to speak) three senior United executives finally apologize to Dave. *Note the contrast between United Airlines' glacially slow and sluggish apology and communication efforts and the speed and agility of Dave Carroll, Taylor Guitars, and Calton Cases.*
>
> **September 22:** Dave speaks at a U.S. Senate hearing on airline passenger rights.

The Stories behind the Story: United Airlines, Taylor Guitars, and Calton Cases

The phenomenon that Dave Carroll created with "United Breaks Guitars" is a textbook example of what I call a World Wide Rave (see my 2009 book with that title), an online chain reaction that takes off when people spread your ideas by repeating your story. And there is much to learn from it if we dig a little deeper.

What Dave achieved is amazing in its own right. But as an observer of these phenomena what fascinates me is the way Taylor Guitars and Calton Cases were able to react in real time to seize the marketing opportunity that Dave's momentum created. On the other hand, United Airlines exhibited a paralysis in the face of a snowballing crisis. In the spread between the small, speedy, and agile players and the slow, clumsy giant I see prima-facie evidence that a revolution has indeed been set in motion.

It's worth taking a closer look at how each of the players reacted.

Break a Taylor Guitar and You Break this Man's Heart

When "United Breaks Guitars" burst on the scene Dave Carroll was already on Taylor Guitar's radar. The El Cajon, California–based guitar maker had featured his band in its owners' magazine, *Wood & Steel*. And having played a

Taylor for 10 years, Dave was a brand devotee—so the song's lyrics weren't about any old guitar getting broken. United broke his *Taylor*.

With lyrics that paid his product such respect, no surprise that Bob Taylor, the guitar-maker's founder and president, heard about it within 24 hours, via a tip from an ex-employee. "I was a fan a tenth of the way through . . . even before he talked about his Taylor guitar," Bob Taylor told me. But as soon as he heard that the damaged instrument was a Taylor, Bob contacted Dave and offered a free replacement. And he didn't stop there.

"I was discussing with our marketing people how we could send a gentle message supporting Dave and the hundreds of others who've had guitars broken on airplanes," Taylor says. "We know this sort of thing happens a lot, and I wanted to let others know 'it's not your fault . . . we feel your pain . . . we can advise you on how to travel safe in future.' We also wanted to let people know that we can fix their instruments."

That's what led Bob to shoot his own YouTube video, "Taylor Guitars Responds to 'United Breaks Guitars.'" Set in the company's service center, the video features no slick production values. "We wanted to convey that we're like family and you're inviting us into your living room," Taylor says. "The idea was to say, 'Hey, we're just people, too, and we have some resources that can help you.'"

Watching the video, I was struck by its deep sincerity, and when I spoke to Bob I learned why. Taylor Guitars is a personal enterprise. Bob started making guitars in high school and founded the company when he was 19. Thirty-five years later he's still in love with his high-school sweetheart—and that shines through in everything he says.

In his short video, Bob offers tips about how to pack and travel with musical instruments. He told me he's been using video for about 10 years, first for training new hires, more recently for marketing purposes on taylorguitars.com and a YouTube channel.

"If the subject is guitars, I'm comfortable in front of the camera," Bob says. "I did three takes of my 'United Breaks Guitars' video—and the whole thing took about 15 minutes' work for me, plus a few more hours for the people working on the rest: things like the logistics and posting."

While the Transportation Security Administration (TSA) and the American Federation of Musicians (AFM) came to an agreement to allow guitars to be considered as carry-on luggage in 2003, thousands of musicians can relate a personal tale of instrument mistreatment at the hands of any number of airlines.

Know the pertinent policies of the airline on which you are traveling. Print them out and take them with you. Many flight attendants do not know their own airline's policy regarding carry-on guitars, so if you can calmly explain that your instrument is within their mandated guidelines, and actually show them those guidelines, you will be way ahead of the game.

The Taylor Guitars' video response to "United Breaks Guitars" was quickly seen by hundreds of thousands of YouTube viewers, and more than 500 viewers left positive ratings and comments. Given the informational content of the video (guitar travel and repair), most viewers were likely professional musicians: Taylor's core market.

To me, that's an impressive return on investment: less than one day's work yields several minutes of detailed attention from, as of this writing, nearly a half million core customers—all because Taylor was alert and agile enough to seize a real-time marketing opportunity: the fleeting moment when Dave Carroll's video was all the rage.

While working on this book, I was struck by how few marketers are prepared to move as fast as Taylor Guitars did. Even if they spotted the chance, most companies would still be discussing it when the window closed.

So why was Bob Taylor able to act so fast?

A Teachable Moment

Although Taylor Guitars had been talking about the proper care and handling of guitars for years, customers tend to ignore such advice—along with everything else found in the back of an owner's manual. So Bob Taylor immediately saw Dave Carroll's experience as an ideal platform on which to build a sense of urgency around a key topic.

Bob was among the first to see "United Breaks Guitars," which had then racked up only 5,000 YouTube views.

"I saw it as a teachable moment because so many people were talking about guitars on airplanes," Taylor says. "We already knew you have to jump on opportunities to communicate when something happens, because it is too late when it is over. And since Dave used video, we figured that was the way for us to tell our story, too."

Taylor's team had already shot many videos, so they were able to act fast once the decision was made. They already had a YouTube video channel in place.

"We don't wait for the stars to align, we just shoot it quickly. It's just a grassroots sort of thing. We just wanted to talk to our peeps while they are enjoying Dave's video."

He may not wait for the stars to align, but Taylor has learned to spot rare opportunities that arise when stars take his product on stage.

"There are very few times something happens that takes our brand forward a few steps," Taylor says. "Newscasters were saying Dave's guitar was a Taylor guitar. I've been doing this for 35 years, and only about a dozen times has something this big come our way . . . like when Taylor Swift began to play Taylor Guitars on stage. When luck turns your way, you can't squander it. Thanks to Dave, now many more people know Taylor guitars. This was a big branding leap for Taylor Guitars."

Case Study in Real-Time Product Development

Dave Carroll's predicament was hardly a case Jim Laffoley could fail to notice: Damage to guitars in transit is specifically what his product is designed to prevent. What's more, Dave's Halifax home is three hours down the road from Moncton, New Brunswick, where Laffoley is president of Calton Cases (North America) Inc.

Musicians around the world consider Calton's products among the most secure cases for stringed instruments, from violins to cellos to guitars. And guitar cases are the company's biggest seller. In fact, had Dave Carroll used a Calton Case when "Flying United" he may not have had an issue with the airline.

"Our primary customer is a professional musician," Laffoley told me. "My goal is to get more professional artists as customers. I wanted to put an artist up on a pedestal because artists are the perfect spokespeople for our products."

"On the Tuesday morning, my lawyer called saying that he'd just seen the 'United Breaks Guitars' video," Laffoley says. At the time, the video had about

25,000 views. "So I called Dave and said, 'You are the perfect spokesman for my product,' and he was immediately receptive to working together."

For starters, Laffoley offered to provide Dave with cases for the band's upcoming tour. But the collaboration quickly moved further.

"It took about two days to go from offering a few cases to proposing a custom-branded line of products," Laffoley says. "And Dave saw the value right away."

As the video passed 200,000 YouTube views, the Dave Carroll Traveler's Edition Guitar Case was born. Every hard-shell case is handmade, and available in 16 exterior and 12 interior colors.

"We came up with an aggressive price point to attract people who wanted to get into a Calton case," Laffoley says. "$725, including shipping anywhere in North America."

Dave Carroll is happy because he gets a cut from each sale and his fellow artists are likewise happy because it's priced lower than a regular Calton case. But the only difference from a regular Calton is the custom badge Laffoley created almost overnight.

As a result, the Dave Carroll edition was offered for sale on Calton's web site—and promoted on Dave's site—within days of the YouTube video release.

Sure, it was only a rebadging effort. But in today's corporate world where product-development efforts involve months or years of "process," it is remarkable to see a product go from concept to sale in just days.

"My background is product management," Laffoley says. "So I was able to work quickly. But all I really did was get Dave to agree, change the label, change the price point, and work out distribution. Sales are going well so far. We're selling cases that we never would have sold without the Dave Carroll edition."

United Comes Untied

Although Dave Carroll's video was making United baggage handlers famous for the wrong reasons, everyone *but* United Airlines was working to seize the moment. Dave was all over the media worldwide. Bob Taylor was teaching musicians how to safeguard and fix their prized instruments. And Jim Laffoley was seizing the moment with a custom-branded guitar case.

Meanwhile, United said absolutely nothing in public. Its PR staff provided no explanation on the corporate web site, offered no statement to the media, and posted no comments on the many blogs that (like mine) talked up the video. In other words, they did not react in real time.

By failing to do so, United missed a huge opportunity to dampen and deflect criticism before it snowballed—and a chance to present a sympathetic, humane face to its customers. Instead of doing something interesting and creative—like a YouTube video of all their baggage handlers bowing in apology, Japanese-style—United chose stony silence. This was just the first of countless opportunities the airline missed. Or how about this as a response—what if United had made a "suitcase camera" that recorded the journey a bag makes at O'Hare as it goes from one plane, through the bowels of the airport baggage system and onto another plane. The video could be sped up to about a minute and narrated by the chief baggage handler. Now that would have generated positive, real-time attention!

United did try to make amends behind the scenes by contacting Dave—but even this effort was ham-handed. "They did not say that they were sorry," Dave recalls. "They did say it was *regrettable*, and they offered some compensation—only because I'm a *good customer* and not because of the video. But I said from the outset that if I had to go the video route, I wouldn't accept compensation personally; that they could give the money to another customer with a damage issue."

It took a lot of punishment for the message to sink in, but Dave thinks United may have finally learned from this experience. He's been told that "United Breaks Guitars" is now used in customer-service training to illustrate how quickly things can turn ugly. And on September 14, 2009, he met with senior United Airlines executives in Chicago.

"They were friendly and engaging and actually said that they were sorry," Dave says. "They took responsibility. Although they did not make excuses, they did talk about some of the reasons for the issues. I told them that there should be some clarity about the United policy on guitars and allowing musicians to take guitars on board. While the policy was always there, they did not make it clear, so they have added a link."

Sadly, the nonreaction *in public*—the instinct to ignore a huge online uprising—is still way too common in the corporate world. I've identified many reasons for this behavior, including undue influence by legal departments who fear "saying something that admits responsibility," sheer panic among frontline staff, bad advice from PR agencies, and executives steeped in a business culture of "no comment."

Although they may have learned something from this, United continues to miss opportunities. As part of my research for this book, on October 7, 2009, I emailed the airline's media relations staff to request an interview. In fairness, I wanted to offer you United's side of the story; to let them tell you what they had learned.

Although my initial email was returned promptly, the media relations staff declined to grant me an interview. And so the damage continues as you read. Does all this make you want to "Fly United"?

Has United Airlines really learned from this disaster? In a similar situation would they now realize the importance of engaging the online dialogue in real time? Would they create their own interesting YouTube video to deflect some of the criticism? Would they take the opportunity to humanize the company and show they care about their passengers?

Dave's Big Win

If United learned and gained nothing from this encounter, the opposite is true for Dave Carroll. His career blossomed under the YouTube spotlight. His band is constantly in demand for live gigs, and listeners buy songs from his web site and iTunes.

"If my guitar had to be smashed due to extreme negligence, I'm glad it was United that did it," Dave says. After more than 8 million views of his videos, Dave jokes, "United broke my career!"

Dave may be famous now, but that was not what he set out to achieve. "My expectations were low," he says. "I was just hoping people at United would see the video and take it seriously."

What made Carroll's video turn into a World Wide Rave while so many others go unnoticed? People I've asked all point to the song itself—which is really good. "I've been working on the songwriting craft for a number of years," Dave says. "The story was laid out well and had hooks in all the right places. But for an independent musician it is tough to get things heard. I don't think the song would have spread without the United Airlines aspects. This song could only have been a success in this particular way."

The song itself was certainly essential, but I'm convinced that Dave's availability to do dozens of media interviews in the hectic first days of the song's release that pushed the video from a few hundred thousand views to several million views in just a few days. In other words, Dave's real-time media relations effort was essential to the viral explosion of the video.

Sudden success has taken Dave's career through many unexpected turns. Having successfully reinvented his personal brand in real time, like it or not, he will be known forever as "that United Breaks Guitars guy." But it's a role he is eager to play.

"Everybody knows this song," he says. "It's the perfect door opener. And now I'm even getting asked to speak about customer service at corporate events."

Dave has also become an unlikely spokesperson for airline passenger rights, having testified at the September 2009 U.S. Senate hearings on the issue. "I'm recognized all the time now when I fly with my guitar," he says. "Many musicians contact me to thank me about drawing attention to the challenge of traveling with guitars. After all, we're talking about our livelihood."

Real-Time Engagement

Real-time marketing.
Real-time product development.
Real-time communication.
Real-time customer service.

What can we learn from a Dave versus Goliath contest in which one irate Canadian musician utterly and completely whips one of the largest marketing and customer-service operations in the United States? What gives when a single improvising amateur can defeat an outfit that should be one of the most sophisticated of its kind on the planet? And how was it that two other small players were able to ride the victor's momentum?

The answer is that the rules have changed. The balance of power has been irrevocably altered.

> Scale and media buying power are no longer a decisive advantage. What counts today is speed and agility.

It takes speed and agility, plus the kind of creative imagination and craft skill that allowed Dave Carroll to write a song every bit as powerful as a Stinger missile.

It takes quick thinking and guts to put your organization out there, to react to events in real-time like Bob Taylor did. But the rewards can be huge. As this book was being finished, Taylor Guitars was working hard to keep up with market demand. The company is making a record number of guitars, nearly 25 percent more than the highest production level in 2008. So a real-time mind-set can affect the bottom line.

If you run a huge business like United Airlines, this should scare the living corn flakes out of you. Perhaps this should cause you to reflect on whether combining two huge bureaucracies in search of greater scale solves your problem or magnifies it.

If you're big, this should scare you—but it need not cause you to lose heart. Whether you run a one-person start-up or a vast global enterprise, you have an equal opportunity to grow by engaging the world around you in real time.

In the chapters to follow we take a practical look at what it takes to win in this new environment. And yes, as you'll see in Chapter 5 large organizations also win . . . if they know what to do.

2

Speed versus Sloth

Dispatches from the Front

In Chapter 1 we saw how real-time public relations and marketing savvy allowed one man to run rings around a clumsy airline giant. In this chapter we look at further evidence that a real-time revolution is profoundly shifting the balance of power.

At 2:20 P.M. Pacific time on June 25, 2009, the entire world learned that Michael Jackson was pronounced dead at the Ronald Reagan UCLA Medical Center. Who flashes the news to a shocked world within minutes? Not the *Los Angeles Times*, not CBS News, not CNN or FOX.

TMZ, an upstart celebrity media news service, got the scoop on this sad tale, immediately posting the story on its web site. As the world learned of Jackson's demise, the now-iconic images of that ambulance featured in media worldwide—each time with the TMZ logo. A player in the news business with fewer than five years' experience, TMZ beat everyone, including local media outlets with many more reporters on the ground.

Why didn't a bigger, more established news outlet get that story first? Why was TMZ among the first to show the world Tiger Woods' damaged Cadillac Escalade? And why was it that TMZ broke the news of Britney Spears's breakup with Kevin Federline?

What's more, at a time when news outlets across America were shrinking dramatically, why was TMZ able to go from zero to $25 million in revenues between 2005 and 2008?

> As media tied to rigid production cycles decline—morning papers, evening newscasts, and weekly newsmagazines—real-time media grow audiences and profits.

Although millions of Americans became news junkies in 2008—glued to one of the most contested elections in U.S. history—conventional news media continued to decline.

Meanwhile, Politico.com, another upstart, carved a new real-time niche at the center of American political discourse—drawing a rapt audience of political players, political junkies, and reporters.

Launched by former *Washington Post* reporters in the run-up to the 2008 U.S. election, Politico grew rapidly on the strength of quick, Web-based reporting of electoral developments. In America's brief electoral off-season Politico has held its audience with quick and comprehensive coverage of the health-care reform battle and other polarizing issues. And its core audience is passionate about American politics. By 2009 *Vanity Fair* reported that Politico had gone from zero to 100 staff at a time when other news outlets were cutting back.

Why didn't the *Washington Post* itself start Politico.com—instead of journalists who had left the company?

The answer to all these questions on both TMZ and Politico boils down to the same thing. Both upstarts understand the advantages that flow from delivering real-time content that satisfies intensely focused public curiosity. Whether curiosity is focused on things that really matter or Lady Gaga, there is money to be made satisfying it in real time.

Nothing attracts curiosity more powerfully or consistently than information that can generate profit. And that's why—as we saw in the Prologue—the real-time revolution came first in finance.

No surprise, then, to find a company that grew in sync with the financial revolution, from zero in 1981 to $6.5 billion revenue in 2008, now leads growth among global media titans.

Bloomberg was a pioneer in delivering real-time news and data to financial markets. And the company continues to grow—going into TV and buying media properties like *BusinessWeek*—while other media conglomerates are in terminal decline. Founder Michael Bloomberg even managed to take over an entire city—having become mayor of New York.

It was real-time strength that propelled Bloomberg past the likes of CBS and Time Life to become the superpower of New York–based media. In this, Bloomberg represents the triumph of "new media" over old—but even among new media, real-time savvy is not a given.

Google Finally Gets It

Even though they get out of bed three hours later than we do, Californians like to think they are ahead of us stuffy Easterners. But it was not until late 2009—as this chapter was being written—that Google, the Godzilla of Silicon Valley, discovered what is bred in Bloomberg's DNA. It's gotta be real time!

Although a carrier rather than a producer, Google is a news medium. But until recently it was not a real-time medium. It was only in late 2009 that Google announced that real-time results will finally be included in searches. What this means is that live updates from sites like Twitter and FriendFeed, plus headlines from news and blog posts, now appear in Google Web Search results mere seconds after they are posted.

Can I share a secret?

When I saw this news I was so excited that my pulse began to race. A chill went up my spine with the realization I was witnessing a key turning point in online history. So I dropped everything to delve into this new development.

The news of Google's real-time search innovation came to me from several people I follow on Twitter. As soon as I saw it I jumped over to Google News Search looking for news stories on the Google announcement. To my dismay, I found a slew of stories up already. Dang! Having been holed up in a meeting as the news broke, hours earlier, I missed the chance to write about it before anyone else. But I still wanted to get a post out quickly.

So I started with Google's official blog, where the announcement had been made. There I found that the real-time features are based on new search technologies that enable Google to monitor more than a billion documents and process hundreds of millions of real-time updates each day.

Google had earlier announced a content-provision partnership with Twitter. But in concert with the real-time search rollout, I found that Google announced similar new tie-ups with Facebook, MySpace, FriendFeed, Jaiku, and Identi.ca—all key players in the real-time social networking world.

I was pleased to learn the search engineers had added "hot topics" to Google Trends. This allows users to spot, in real time, the topics most widely discussed online. These trending phrase lists (a standard feature of Twitter from early on) are critical because this is how you spot emerging trends and patterns.

The announcement of this development on its blog was further evidence that Google was starting to get real time. That meant the news was disseminated quickly, as people instantly tweeted and then blogged their take on its significance.

Breaking news on company sites and blogs is an important real-time technique because it gives your greatest supporters first access to the information. This also allows for comments and clarifications to be made in real time as questions come in. We discuss this strategy in detail later in the book.

The real-time search announcement was significant because it signals that our friends at the Googleplex finally realize the importance of real-time media. Prior to this innovation I had long felt the lack of real-time search limited the value of the Google search engine.

For several years, I found it odd that I had to go to three places (owned by two different companies) to search for the information I needed. I used Google to search for news and to scan the Web for content more than a few days old. But I relied on Twitter searches (and services like TweetDeck) to find what's up right now. Now I can see it all on Google.

Google's innovation came as recognition that it is critically important for businesses to hear what people are saying in real time. Finally, here was the pair of ears United Airlines lacked in dealing with Dave Carroll.

Caught on the News Cycle Hamster Wheel

Why do upstarts like TMZ, Politico, and Bloomberg now beat the likes of *People* magazine, the *Washington Post*, and *Newsweek*? At a time when Americans are consuming unprecedented volumes of news and information online, why did more than 15,000 people across the United States lose their newspaper jobs in 2009?

I would argue that focusing on real time is critical to achieving a sustainable business model in media.

So why can't incumbent media companies make the jump to real time?

My own view is that these organizations are burdened by cultural habits deeply ingrained by their manufacturing processes, by the news cycles they follow. For newspapers it's the daily print deadline. For TV news, it's the prime time broadcast. When the opportunity to move online arose, for these organizations it was an afterthought. And because online was an afterthought it did not force the core culture to reinvent itself.

> Huge advantage flows from delivering in real-time content that satisfies intensely focused public curiosity.

Meanwhile, companies that started from scratch with a real-time mind-set continue to grow—and not only in the news business. Across the economy, people are finding success by understanding the power of *now*. The power of real time is at work in your business, too.

Feeling an Invisible Presence in the Conference Hall

Conferences are a medium and business quite distinct from the news media. And the conference business is experiencing the real-time revolution in an altogether different way.

The conference as we used to know it was stiff, structured, and didactic. It's been the same since Cicero—the speaker spoke and the audience listened. Maybe the audience had a chance to ask questions at the end, or chat about the content at coffee break, but like television it was essentially one-way communication.

People who speak at conferences for a living, like me, had cause to wonder if live events would disappear. But then something interesting happened. The ploddingly slow physical-event business picked up some real-time speed.

Now, at conferences all over the world, audience members connect with one another in real time while speakers are up at the podium. This "back-channel" is truly revolutionary because it allows listeners to discuss content as it is being delivered. What's more, it brings a new virtual audience into the room—sometimes from the opposite end of the Earth.

Using hashtags (unique identifiers used by Twitter users to mark and locate tweets) people in the audience and everywhere else can tune into the back channel. Many attendees post photos and video clips in real time, too, so people can see what's happening.

As a consequence, closed events are now open to the world. Good presentations get instant rave reviews and bad ones get panned just as fast.

Today, when I lead panel discussions I frequently take questions both from the audience and via Twitter. At one gig in Boston, I received a question from New Zealand, which I then asked the live audience.

Sometimes the back chat does get frivolous—like the tweeting about my choice of belt at one recent gig. But much of the stream is more valuable than what's holding up my trousers. For example, people often tweet links to online resources relevant to the topic at the moment the speaker is talking about it.

I have also seen the Twitter back channel generate immediate sales. As I spoke at an event in Amsterdam, local bookseller Danielle Shouten tweeted a link to a special deal on my book, *The New Rules of Marketing & PR*. How cool is that?

It's not just Twitter either. Some people at conferences now use GPS-enabled mobile applications like Foursquare—which allows you to see where your friends are in the conference hall (or playing hooky at the bar). And with live video streaming services like Qik, anyone can upload a speech to the Internet in real time.

What Matters Now

Even in book publishing, the oldest and most traditional of media, people are finding creative new ways to harness the power of now.

In late 2009, Seth Godin asked 70 people, whom he describes as "big thinkers," to contribute a one-page essay with a one-word title. These he brought together in a free e-book: *What Matters Now*. Contributors included bestselling authors Elizabeth Gilbert and Tom Peters, tech thinkers Kevin Kelly and Guy Kawasaki, and publishers Tim O'Reilly and Arianna Huffington.

As Godin kindly included my essay "Attention" in the e-book, I knew when it was coming, I got an insider's chance to watch and measure a real-time online phenomenon in the making.

What Matters Now was released on Godin's blog at 5 A.M. EST on December 14, 2009. Contributors were asked to keep it quiet until release time, and then to blog and tweet about it simultaneously. So, along with other contributors, I preset a blog post to send automatically at precisely 5 A.M.

Within an hour *What Matters Now* was one of the top phrases on Twitter—a so-called "trending topic." People were tweeting and retweeting like crazy (a retweet is when you forward somebody else's tweet to your followers), at one point reaching a rate of more than one tweet per second. Many people also began leaving comments on the contributors' blog posts.

Soon after, blog posts from beyond the group of contributors began to appear. In a case like this, bloggers often compete to set the agenda for discussion by trying to get the first word in, posting before anyone else.

> Just as a bond trader makes money by trading first, bloggers strive to set the agenda by being the first to share something big with readers.

Since Seth Godin is a very influential marketing thinker, and because he brought dozens of other thought leaders into the project, many others wanted to share these ideas on their own blogs, and quickly. So in a race to be first the number of blog posts followed a predictable pattern.

On release day, 119 blog posts mentioned *What Matters Now*, according to an analysis I did in association with Dow Jones, using their Insight product. On the second day there were 90 posts; 48 on the third and 27 on the fourth day. After that, the number of posts trailed off steeply.

This follows a predictable pattern, which we look at in detail in Chapter 3. For the following three weeks, an average of five posts a day mentioned *What Matters Now*. And even months later the e-book was still mentioned a few times daily.

"There's a power law of attention at work online," Seth Godin told me soon after the release of *What Matters Now*. "A lot of the people working (for free and for pay) online are in the Jimmy-Olsen, scoop-the-competition business.

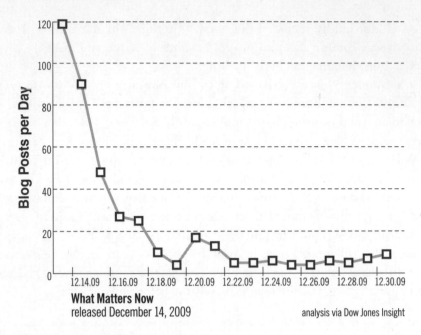

What Matters Now
released December 14, 2009

analysis via Dow Jones Insight

What Matters Now: Blog Posts per Day

Because news travels so fast, being first is everything. I wasn't at all surprised to see *What Matters Now* spike, because we planned for that. With dozens of authors breaking the news at once, we lit the news match in a lot of places, and the kindling caught."

Can You See the Pattern?

From Dave Carroll and his broken guitar through Seth Godin and his instant-hit e-book, I see patterns that appear again and again throughout the real-time online world.

I have shared all the stories you have read from the Prologue to this point because to me these real-life examples reveal that change is underway—and patterns and mechanisms are at work.

Remember the stories so far, because in Chapter 3 we take a look at the new patterns, the new mechanisms, and the new laws at work throughout this body of experience. Then, in Chapter 4, we look at the attitudes and the mind-sets that can help your organization adapt to a new reality.

3 Laying Down Some Real-Time Law

Now that we find ourselves in a real-time revolution, businesspeople are feeling their way forward in search of new truths. The laws have changed. The road signs are gone. It's like trying to drive across America with a map made in 1950, before the Interstate system. On the ground you can hardly find a trace of Route 66!

That's what this book is about. It's an aid to navigation designed to take you into unmapped territory. It digs into how companies, nonprofits, government agencies, entrepreneurs, and even jobseekers can reach their goals by getting the *first* word in every conversation with customers and clients— responding to what they say *as they say it.*

Clearly, consumers understand that saving time is a key advantage of the Web. One quick Google search now delivers in seconds the research that used to take hours in a library. Where comparison shopping used to be local and required driving all over town, or thumbing through the Yellow Pages, today, it's global and instantaneous.

> The Internet has fundamentally changed the pace of business, compressing time and rewarding speed.

It is much harder to find evidence that business has grasped the gravity of this shift and adapted internal processes to the new pace. In fact, marketing,

PR, communications, product development, and customer support now look much like 1950s cars on a modern expressway, crawling along the slow lane at speeds for which they were designed.

Let's resist the temptation just to honk at them for blocking traffic. Better to explain patiently—because it does get technical—just how modern speed limits work.

The New Laws on Speed

There are now multiple dimensions to the speed of communications.

The ideal *tempo* is natural, the pace of real people talking in conversation. If you asked someone a question, wouldn't it disturb you if they stared back blankly for an hour before answering? That's easy to understand.

What is harder to get your head around is the scope of conversation and the speed at which it now expands, flows, and contracts.

Seemingly out of nowhere millions of people join a conversation about a guy whose guitar got broken. Across millions, the focus of the conversation suddenly shifts in response to new information. Then, as quickly as it started, the chatter fades to nearly zero.

What's happening here? How does this work?

There are two "laws" that govern how news spreads online. They are not new laws. They have been used for many years to describe observable phenomena. They may have been on your high school science exam. But they dictate the speed at which we now need to engage the market: the *power law* and the *law of normal distribution*.

The Real-Time Power Law

The power law concept turns up again and again both in nature and human endeavors. It governs the distribution of data where a large concentration (a "spike") of events is followed by a quick drop off to a "long tail" of continuing but less frequent events.

In nature, the size of craters on the moon follows the power law pattern. If we plot the size of the craters against the number of craters of each size, we see a spike representing the few very large craters (miles wide) trailing off quickly to the long tail of millions of tiny craters.

The popularity of web sites is a good man-made example. A few extremely popular sites like Google and Wikipedia get millions of visitors per day, but

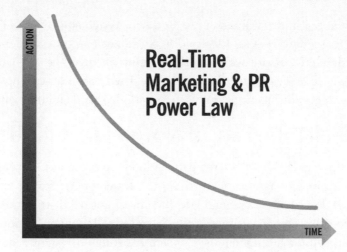

Real-Time Marketing & PR Power Law

the traffic pattern quickly trails off to the millions of sites that only get a handful of visitors per day.

In the context of this book, the power law governs the dissemination of breaking news in a real-time environment. That's why I call it the "Real-Time Marketing & PR Power Law."

I first saw this "law" working on Wall Street, as mentioned in the Prologue. Most large-volume trading activity occurred in the first few seconds after news broke that the Federal Reserve entered the market. That's when the big players did their trades. Although the news affected trading all day, most of the activity was immediate.

The same thing happens as people are affected by shocking news. When the World Trade Center fell, John Lennon was shot, and JFK was assassinated, everyone remembers exactly what they were doing at that moment.

Online, the number of story "occurrences" spikes quickly as news breaks. That is followed by a quick trail-off in the rate at which stories are produced. On the day Michael Jackson died, thousands of real-time news stories were posted to online news sites and blogs in just the first several hours.

Understanding and heeding this law is critical. If you don't, when something important happens in your backyard it will be over before you even react. You've got to react quickly to the news; if not first, then early not late.

From the bond traders (described in the Prologue), I learned that once the news is out all over, the chance to profit is gone. From Lou Crandall, chief economist at real-time Wall Street research firm Wrightson ICAP, LLC (where I worked in the late 1980s), I learned how instant market commentary and analysis, delivered at precisely the right moment, drives action. And from Seth Godin (as discussed in Chapter 2) I learned how you can harness the power law to get your message out with incredible speed and momentum.

The Real-Time Law of Normal Distribution

Where the power law describes the pattern likely to occur as news of immediate and widespread significance breaks, the trajectory of stories that build over time is described by a second law: the law of normal distribution.

The news that United Airlines broke Dave Carroll's guitar did not stop the world from spinning. But after Dave posted his song on YouTube momentum built slowly until it reached critical mass. Then it trailed off.

Just like the power law, the law of normal distribution is found everywhere in nature and in human endeavors. For example, with body height we see many people clustered around the average and a few very tall or very short people at the edges.

In that example, body height is represented by the *x*-axis (the horizontal one). If we make "time" the *x*-axis, you can expect to see the same law of normal distribution at work with the popularity of a rock band. The band starts small, gains fans over time, peaks, and then trails off in popularity.

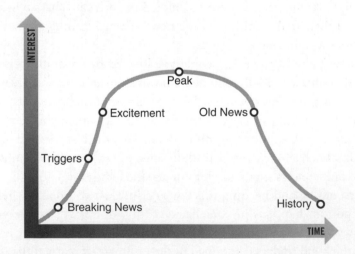

Real-Time Marketing & PR Law of Normal Distribution

We constantly see this phenomenon at work online. One blogger throws off a spark, saying something outrageous or insightful. A few people who notice react with blog posts, tweets, or emails to friends. As people in this second wave begin to discuss the issue momentum starts to build. Eventually, a reporter picks up on the conversation and writes about it in the mainstream media. From that point the story catches fire. As we saw with Dave Carroll's guitar, this is how a World Wide Rave can start.

When a story begins to snowball, the first imperative is to understand which law governs its trajectory: the power law or the law of normal distribution. If the power law has been invoked, you had best prepare for the tsunami to arrive within hours, minutes, or even seconds. But if normal distribution is at work and the story is in its early stages, you may have a wider range of options. Either way, don't sit on your thumbs. The sooner you react the better.

If you consider the typical bell-shaped curve that characterizes the law of normal distribution, there are definite benefits to being quick. People and organizations that react early (during the period of increasing interest) benefit in many important ways:

- When you start the conversation, you are recognized as someone who is plugged into the marketplace of ideas.

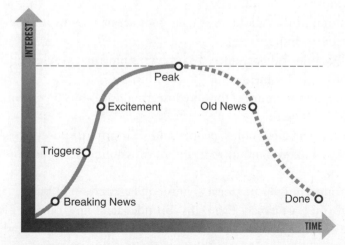

Generating Interest

- If you talk about an idea early, you naturally get more exposure because the threads of conversation stem from what you have said. If you're in late you get lost in the cacophony.
- With a new product, if you are first to market in a hot category, your initial momentum may give you an advantage for many years.
- If you're an early adopter on a social media platform, you build a larger following than those who join later.
- If you're first to engage the market, people notice and your offering gains valuable attention.
- If you react early and connect with customers as their concerns arise, they see you as thoughtful and caring.

How Would *You* React?

Throughout the real-time online world of the Web, we see the same patterns again and again as stories are driven by the power law and the law of normal distribution. This should prompt you and your organization to consider some key questions. Could you recognize a snowballing situation in its early stages?

How would you react if, *right now* . . . ?

- Your company is cited as "the best place to work" by your local newspaper.
- A customer raves about your customer service on an influential trade magazine web site.
- A well-known industry analyst says on his blog that your company is too difficult to do business with.
- A competitor announces they are lowering prices by 25 percent.
- Your CEO is fired.
- In forums and chat rooms, people said your product poses a health risk.
- A huge company announces its intent to acquire your competitor.

Be they opportunities or threats, you may be confronted by scenarios like these when you least expect them. If you understand how quickly events can unfold and are ready to react, you will gain significant competitive advantage.

The key, as we see in Chapter 4, is having the right mind-set.

4 Real-Time Attitude

What sorts of attitudes and behaviors does it take to move up the ladder in your organization?

If you work for a large company, chances are upward momentum favors steady qualities like compliance, caution, and consensus over speedy traits like imagination, initiative, and improvisation. That's the nature of the beast. Big business is designed to move forward according to plan, at a measured and deliberate pace.

Back when the attention and obedience of consumers could be bought with media advertising, this worked reasonably well. Big business was able to set the pace.

Today, though, with only limited guidance from mass media, consumers set the pace. Left to their own devices, they imagine all sorts of things. They take unpredictable initiatives. They improvise all over the map at high speed.

Having for generations selectively bred such rash traits out of the corporate DNA, it now takes a huge and deliberate effort for big business to adopt a real-time, customer-driven mind-set. Most large companies can't even get their heads around the idea.

Business as Usual

I've talked with people all over the world who are wrestling with the challenge, and most are not at all comfortable with adopting a real-time mind-set. It's not on the corporate agenda or the business-school curriculum. And when the notion is put to them, many people dismiss quick response to opportunities and threats as "reckless" or "risky."

Attitudes are so ingrained that even when confronted with an iceberg off the bow, companies persist in choosing slow and cautious over quick and nimble. Way too much time is spent checking, getting permission, researching, and running it past "experts." By the time a decision is finally reached it's time to head for the lifeboats.

What's Expected in the Corporate World

- Wait, to make certain.
- Work from checklists dictated by one-year and even five-year business plans.
- Measure results quarterly.
- Execute based on a long-term "new product launch" mentality.
- Organize around multimonth marketing and communications "campaigns."
- Get permission from your superior.
- Run decisions by your staff.
- Bring in the experts, the agencies, and the lawyers.
- Conduct extensive research.
- Carefully evaluate all the alternatives.
- Aim for perfection before public release.
- Respond to customers on *your* time frame.
- Engage with media, analysts, and commentators only when convenient and comfortable for *you*.

None of this is inherently wrong. Clearly, research, planning, and teamwork are essential. The problem is that speed and agility are too often sacrificed for the sake of "process." To overcome that you need to consciously and proactively adopt a real-time mind-set.

The Real-Time Mind-Set

The real-time mind-set recognizes the importance of *speed*. It is an attitude to business (and to life) that emphasizes *moving quickly* when the time is right.

Developing a real-time mind-set is not an *either/or* proposition. I'm not saying you should abandon your current business-planning process. Nor do

I advocate allowing your team to run off barking at every car that drives by. Focus and collaboration are essential.

The smart answer is to adopt a *both/and* approach, covering the spectrum from thorough to nimble. Recognize when you need to throw the playbook aside, and develop the capacity to react quickly.

> An immensely powerful competitive advantage flows to organizations with people who understand the power of real-time information.

Developing that capacity requires sustained effort: encouraging people to take initiative; celebrating their success when they go out on a real-time limb; cutting them slack when they try and fail. None of this is easy.

Real-Time Business

- Act before the window of opportunity vanishes.
- Revise plans as the market changes.
- Measure results today.
- Execute based on what's happening now.
- Implement strategies and tactics based on breaking news.
- Empower your people to act.
- Move when the time is right.
- Encourage people to make wise decisions quickly, alone if necessary.
- Make swift inquiries, but be prepared to act.
- Quickly evaluate the alternatives and choose a course of action.
- Get it done and push it out, because it will never be perfect.
- Respond to customers on *their* time frames.
- Engage with media at the moment *they* need your input.

No More Business as Usual

The process starts with an understanding of just how severely conventional methods can handicap business functions—especially marketing and PR—in the always-on world of instant communication.

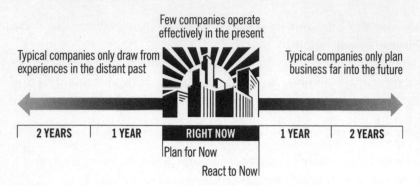

Few companies operate
effectively in the present

Typical companies only draw from
experiences in the distant past

Typical companies only plan
business far into the future

| 2 YEARS | 1 YEAR | RIGHT NOW | 1 YEAR | 2 YEARS |

Plan for Now

React to Now

Business Planning Process

The conventional approach favors a "campaign" (note the war meta-phor) that requires people to spend weeks or months planning to hit "tar-gets." Agencies must be consulted. Messaging strategies must be developed. Advertising space/time must be bought. Conference rooms and refreshments must be prepared for press conferences. Do you serve them sushi or sandwiches?

In planning ahead, marketing and PR teams commonly look back. What were we doing five or six quarters ago? What happened at the trade show last year? In doing so they ignore what's happening right now, today, this instant.

It's a comfortable way to work, following the plan and the process. Just do what's expected and there is no risk of getting in trouble. By contrast, responding to events in real time is uncomfortable; it requires quick thinking and taking risks.

So Why Bother?

- Because now events unfold light years faster than a conventional campaign can deal with.
- Because your nimble, real-time-oriented competitor may snatch a huge opportunity from under your nose before you even notice it's there.
- Because your company will look out of touch and clueless when a crisis hits and you have nothing to say for a whole hour.
- Because one single customer, whose broken guitar your people neglected, may rock your world.

It's Not the Tools, It's the Mind-Set Behind Them

It's easy to dodge the real issue by making a real-time fashion statement. When an executive vice president corners you to say, "I just read this book on real-time marketing and PR . . . so what are we doing to get with it?" you can respond, "We've now got a Facebook page, a YouTube channel, and we tweet on average 2.5 times a day."

Unless and until your company gets caught up in an online firestorm, you can probably get by just showing you've got the tools. And you can find all types of self-proclaimed social-media gurus who will tell you it's all about the tools.

Sure Twitter et al. are important. But it's not about the tools. It's about adapting your mind-set to the new environment these tools create.

> Social media are tools. Real time is a mind-set.

If you want to do more than pretend you get it, you need transform your organization on several levels.

For Individuals, Communicating in Real Time Comes Naturally

When it comes to developing a real-time mind-set, a one-man business like mine has a huge advantage over any big business. If you ask me a question, I don't have to consult a higher authority before answering. (Well, unless the answer affects weekend plans; then I have to ask my wife and daughter.) In the pages ahead, you will find lots more advice for one-person businesses, but bear with me while I help the slow-learners.

The larger the business the more difficult it is to adopt a real-time mind-set. People must be empowered to think on the fly, to take initiative, and to use common sense, empathy, and judgment derived from experience—all stuff that's *verboten* in most companies.

Occasionally you encounter customer-service people who have not yet had these qualities beaten out of them. Hearing a customer's dilemma over the phone, they will go "off-script" to solve the problem on the spot, favoring empathy and common sense over the rulebook. Sadly, these customer-service heroes are so rare that every time one of them saves the day customers come away loving the company they work for. Internally, though, these kind souls are too often seen as misfits. The automatons get promoted.

As Seth Godin discusses in his book *Linchpin*, motivated people don't wait to be told what to do. People who bring flexibility and humanity to their work are the ones best positioned to thrive in today's economy. Successful people plan for the future and have long-term goals, but at the same time they recognize you can't plan for everything: unforeseen opportunities and threats can arise at any moment.

To develop a real-time mind-set, cultivate individuals for whom it is second nature.

But Large Organizations Need to Work At It

The more people you have in an organization, the tougher it is to communicate in real time. In a command-and-control environment where no action can be taken without authority, without consultation, without due process, any individual who shows initiative can expect to be squashed.

The challenge is to develop a new balance that empowers employee initiative but offers real-time guidance when it's needed—like a hotline to higher authority.

Some companies are making good progress at this. And one good indicator is whether employees are allowed to do real-time social networking on the job. If your company *blocks* access to Facebook or Twitter, you do *not* work for a business with a real-time mind-set.

Companies that do have a real-time mind-set push decision making as far down the ladder as possible. Frontline service reps decide how best to deal with customer issues. Marketers are free to blog about their work and comment on other people's blogs as appropriate. Public relations staffers are empowered to respond immediately, without asking management or the lawyers.

In a real-time corporate culture everyone is recognized as a responsible adult.

And Leaders Need to Make It Happen

If you're the leader, and you want to cultivate a real-time mind-set throughout your organization, tear down the command-and-control mentality. Recognize your employees as responsible adults. Empower them to take initiative. Give them opportunities to hone their communication skills and, like IBM, give them clear guidelines as to what's appropriate and what's not.

It's at the bottom of the ladder that change needs to happen. But the impetus can only come from the top. And for leaders, this adds another imperative to the three questions famously posed by management theorist Peter Drucker:

1. *What is your business?*
2. *Who is your customer?*
3. *What does your customer consider value?*

Today, you should also ask: How can we deliver value faster?

5 Too Big to Succeed?

Are some companies too big to fail? That's been a hot question in recent years. But when talking about the revolution in real time, you need to turn this question around: Are some companies too big to *succeed*? With epochal changes underway, are the largest enterprises, like dinosaurs, too unwieldy to evolve? It's a scary question that needs to be asked.

In Chapter 4 I discussed how real-time communications comes naturally to individuals and small teams. But in a large beast is it possible for new information to travel fast enough from tail to skull and back again? Will the response be inevitably robotic? Is there any evidence that the majors are indeed evolving? After these questions sparked heated discussion among my friends I thought I'd better do some quick diagnostics. But how could I do that?

After mulling this over, it occurred to me that the top 100 U.S. companies was as good a focus group as any. So I used the *Fortune* 500, the annual list from *Fortune* magazine that ranks by gross revenue America's top 500 public corporations. Happily, the latest list was issued on May 3, 2010, as I was finishing up the manuscript for this book.

I sent an inquiry via email to the media relations department of each of the top 100 companies on the list. I asked each company to tell me how it had adapted to the new realities of the real-time Web. Here's what I asked:

Hello,

    I would be grateful if you would please forward this inquiry on to the most appropriate person for response.

I am researching a story that will appear first on my blog. I am likely to also publish what I learn in an article under my byline in the *Huffington Post* and in a book I am currently writing due out in November 2010.

I am reaching out to other companies as well.

QUESTION: In the last year or two, has the structure of your corporate communications team and/or communications processes changed to embrace the real-time digital era? If so, how?

A sentence to a paragraph is fine as a response.

Many thanks,

David

I included my email signature with a link to my site, blog, and Twitter ID in case people wanted to find out more about me right away.

I heard back from 28 of the *Fortune* 100 companies. In itself, that top-line result is not encouraging evidence that the lights are on in corporate America. Even more discouraging was the tone-deaf response from many who did reply. On the other hand, it was very encouraging to find that a few companies are already very much on the ball. That leads me to hope the others will be able to catch up once they focus on the right questions.

Here are some highlights from what I learned. Note that some of these strategies will sound familiar as you read on in the book—which I take as evidence that it's not just hip California start-ups and Canadian musicians that communicate in real time.

I'll start with a story from an aerospace company, to whose products I entrust my life several times a month. Believe me: I was relieved to find these guys are awake in the cockpit.

Boeing's Radar Belatedly Spots Harry's Plane

Harry Winsor, an eight-year-old from Boulder, Colorado, loves airplanes so much that he's drawn hundreds of them. So he sent one of his favorites, rendered in crayon, to Boeing. Imagine his disappointment when Boeing responded with a cold form letter stating that they do not accept unsolicited ideas.

That prompted Harry's father John to write a blog post titled, "Is Your Customer Service Ready for the New World of Openness?" He attached Harry's drawing and Boeing's form letter, and invited his readers to comment. To get the word out, he tweeted a link to the post.

If this story was about most other large organizations, it would end there. You would have a disappointed kid, a father ready to strangle the corporate drone who sent the letter, and a bunch of people who read about it online shaking their heads at the mega-corporate folly.

But when Todd Blecher, communications director at Boeing, saw the tweet he responded immediately to Harry's dad and his followers (using the Twitter ID @BoeingCorporate). *The letter Mr. Winsor posted is, as he said, a required response. For kids, we can do better. We'll work on it,* Blecher tweeted.

Work on it Blecher did. He called Harry and spoke to him about the drawing. And he insisted on the need for a better way for Boeing to handle letters from children. After Blecher's quick response, there was an immediate and positive reaction from people who had followed the saga online.

"We're focused on engaging in the digital space and trying to put a human face on the company," Blecher told me. Boeing employs a team of communicators who monitor the real-time Web and are empowered to respond quickly. "We've had a mind-set shift. Leadership has understood that we need to go all-in and be responsive."

Boeing, as I discovered, is one of few *Fortune* 100 companies proactively adapting to the real-time challenge. Let's look at some of the other responses (and nonresponses) to my inquiry.

Build a Team

"Our structures and processes around public relations, marketing, and customer service evolved as a result of the real-time digital era," Joe Strupek told me. Strupek is the assistant vice president for public affairs at State Farm Insurance. "We built a cross-departmental team to develop and implement a strategy, aligned dedicated resources to monitoring and joining in conversations, and all our communications—internal and external—take real-time digital into consideration. But more importantly, it changed our way of thinking. Real-time digital created a heightened sense of awareness around the influence consumers have and helped us focus on the benefits of communicating directly with the public, to share ideas so we can better meet their needs."

Coca-Cola sees the global communications' landscape changing dramatically. "There has been a convergence and blurring of lines between traditional 'communications' and 'marketing,'" says Petro Kacur, senior manager, marketing communications at the Coca-Cola Company. "This has changed our view of the communications function and how we engage with our consumers. We are moving from a monologue to a dialogue. In recognition of these growing trends and their impact on our company's reputation, in March 2009 we formed an office of digital communications and social media. [This office] will help us become even more comfortable and effective in these new spaces."

At Chevron, as at other *Fortune* 100 companies including Intel and Ford Motor, an individual has been charged with leadership in this new area. Justin Higgs, media advisor for policy, government, and public affairs at Chevron Corporation, has been in his role for two years.

Monitor What's Being Said

As we will see in Chapter 8, companies that are adapting to the real-time Web actively monitor what's being said about them using social Web analytics. Verizon Communication's approach is typical: "Over the last two years, we have dramatically stepped up our involvement in social and online media, recognizing that the media landscape has shifted exponentially," Peter Thonis, chief communications officer at Verizon Communications told me. "We've reorganized to monitor this online world and to be able to respond quickly, as well as to engage proactively when we want to tell our story or announce new products. Today, we have multiple communications professionals who work the digital media full time, and every member of our team is involved at some level."

Wells Fargo was the first major bank to have a blog and dedicated social media team, starting in 2006. "We want to be where our customers are," says Ed Terpening, VP and manager of social media at Wells Fargo. "A good example of this is our Twitter handle, @Ask_WellsFargo. We are able to find opportunities to offer help to customers that need it and thank customers for their business by listening to the Twittersphere for mentions of Wells Fargo. Tools like Twitter provide us real-time insight into consumer sentiment and news related to our businesses."

Develop Guidelines and Train Staff

As we will see in Chapter 13, IBM has been a leader in setting guidelines that encourage employees to communicate in real time. Several of the *Fortune* 100 companies I spoke with have developed similar guidelines and training programs for staff. Prudential Finance is a good example.

"We created, and management adopted, a social media policy for employees that was designed around our existing communications policies, recognizing that while the technology may be changing, the company already had sufficient policy governing how employees can communicate externally and internally," Bob DeFillippo, Prudential's chief communications officer, told me.

At Ford Motor, Scott Monty, head of global digital communications, has instituted training for the communications staff to give everyone an understanding of how the real-time Web fits into their job function. This knowledge helps employees start to build real time into their strategic planning as well as their day-to-day interactions.

Intel has created a Social Media Center of Excellence, guidelines, and what they call the "Digital IQ" social-media training with a complete curriculum. "The training brings people up to speed quickly," said Ken E. Kaplan, new media and broadcast manager at Intel. "Anybody can take it, but sales and marketing people are required to take the training. . . . The Digital IQ curriculum for educating employees around the world also includes an internal community to share news, best practices, and key learning."

Engage with the Market

I was encouraged to learn that several *Fortune* 100 companies are engaging the market via the real-time Web—as we saw with Boeing. UPS is equally on the ball. "Like a lot of companies, we've seen great opportunities to connect with our audiences and share information," Debbie Curtis-Magley from UPS public relations told me. "The ability to respond quickly to news occurrences and incorrect information helps us make sure that the media, employees, customers, and the public have access to facts."

In January 2010, UPS and several other brands caught wind of a fast-spreading rumor in social media channels. "It was claimed that UPS was offering free shipping to Haiti for packages under 50 pounds," Curtis-Magley says. "We responded immediately through Twitter and Facebook to correct the rumor and direct people to our company blog, *upside*. The blog story profiled UPS contributions to aid agencies, informed viewers that shipping services were on hold to Haiti, and provided a list of disaster-relief agencies where the public could direct its support. In less than 24 hours, our outreach efforts generated almost 10,000 views of the blog story. During that period, we tracked 38 blogs and discussion forums that corrected the rumor. Statements from our blog were quoted in online news coverage at CNN, *Foreign Policy*, and NPR. Aid agencies also helped get the word out, with the Salvation Army publishing a correction to the UPS rumor at its blog."

As you can see from these responses, for many of the *Fortune* 100, the answer to my original question—*In the last year or two, has the structure of your corporate communications team and/or communications processes changed to embrace the real-time digital era?*—is a definitive "yes."

Thank You for Your Inquiry

Boeing, Chevron, Coca-Cola, Ford, Intel, Prudential Financial, State Farm Insurance, UPS, Verizon Communications, Wells Fargo, and others who answered my questions deserve to be recognized as leaders. So let me say this to any senior managers from those companies who might read this: "Your real-time communications team is doing a great job, please give them a pat on the back from me."

I was amazed when some of these companies responded to me in real time to ask follow-up questions, suggest that we go into depth on the phone, or simply to decline participation. These responses are also useful in the analysis of my little experiment.

Corinne Kovalsky from Raytheon was the fastest responder of all, reaching me just 10 minutes after I emailed her company. She told me she was about to board an airplane and asked about my deadline. Now that's fast! Warren Lee of Marathon Oil responded within two hours to say that the company was in the middle of issuing quarterly earnings that day and he needed more time to get back to me. Wow, that's amazing. A top communications officer of a *Fortune* 100 company takes the time to respond to my inquiry right away, even on the busiest communication day of the quarter.

Several people responded quickly just to say that they wouldn't be able to comment on my inquiry. In fact, the second-fastest response in the *Fortune* 100 came in from Microsoft (15 minutes), and they declined to comment. I also received responses from Travelers Cos. and Kraft Foods declining to participate. Even though they declined to participate, I appreciated that their media representatives were courteous enough to get back to me quickly. That, too, gets points.

I wanted to be scientific about this, and make sure I could measure the response rates I got from the *Fortune* 100. But before I was even able to pose a question, I had to find someone to ask. And this proved to be *much* more difficult than expected.

Contact Us (Or Not)

In my work as a contributing editor for *EContent* magazine, in the articles I write for the *Huffington Post*, and in the course of research for my blog and books like this one, I frequently contact corporate media relations people. I prefer email to the phone. Although some journalists still use the phone to make initial contact, in my experience, way more than 90 percent of first requests come via email, so that's how I approached this research.

The first thing I needed was an email address for each of the 100 companies. I gathered these the week before so that I could send all the emails in one go to be as fair as possible about response times.

Here's the process I went through. I first Googled the exact company name as it appears on the 2010 *Fortune* 500 list. I then went to the media-relations section of each company's web site and looked for an email address. I preferred general addresses (e.g., media@company.com). It turned out that only 26 companies offered a general media-relations email address. My second choice was a Web form, and 14 companies had that option. If I couldn't find either of those, I looked for an individual person to email—although as a journalist I don't like doing this because you never know if that person is traveling or on vacation. If that was the only option, I selected the most senior person or, if the people were organized by department, the one who was most appropriate.

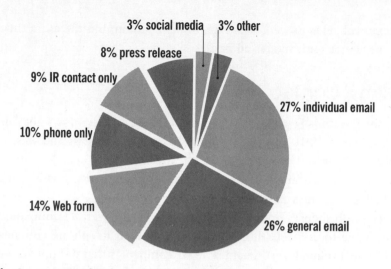

Media Contact Method: *Fortune* 100 Companies

I was happy to find that three companies—AT&T, Hewlett-Packard, and Raytheon—listed email addresses for social-media representatives (and those people got back to me fast). All told, the process yielded 70 contacts and was quite easy. At most companies, I had an email address or form URL in less than one minute.

Then things got much more difficult. On many corporate sites, email addresses for the media-relations team proved impossible to find. So I had to get creative, scanning press releases for email contacts. I found routes into eight companies this way. At nine other companies where no media-relations contact was available I found investor relations contacts, so I used those instead. Although IR is another department, I assumed that they were in constant contact with the PR team and would just forward my inquiry.

Ten companies offered only telephone contacts. Sure, I could have phoned them. But I decided upfront that I wanted to make all initial contacts online. And, hey, I'm writing a book about Web communications here!

In trying to find contact details I had a few annoying experiences. Pfizer offered a form, which is fine, but limited the inquiry to 500 characters, many fewer than I needed for my request. That seems a ridiculous limitation! Hey Pfizer, will you overdose if you ingest more than 500 characters?

The American International Group's form did not work at all when I tried it—broken—hello AIG! And the Walgreens' form required prior registration and approval. This procedure is fine, in my opinion, but the extra time that takes may deter some interested parties.

Making Contact

I sent the inquiries between 1:01 P.M. and 1:44 P.M. Eastern Daylight Time on Tuesday, May 4, 2010 (normal business hours on both east and west coasts of the United States).

So much for the encouraging news; let's move on to Jurassic Park and see which giants show no sign of evolutionary progress.

I received responses from 28 companies, and there were 11 companies that I was unable to contact (those that only provided telephone contacts and AIG with its broken form). That leaves 61 companies that did not answer my inquiry in any way. (See the appendix for a list of the entire 100 companies.)

Some companies sent me a canned form in response:

Massachusetts Mutual Life Insurance: *Thank you. We have received your e-mail and will contact you with a response.* (I got no response.)

Amazon.com: *Thank you for your submission. Your request has been sent. You will receive a response shortly.* (I got no response.)

Walgreens: *Thank you for sending your information request. A site administrator will respond to your request soon.* (Again, no response. And by the way, what's a "site administrator"?)

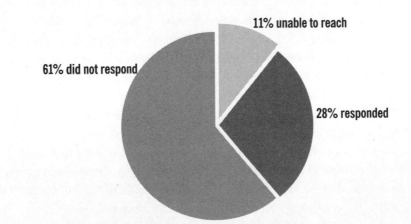

11% unable to reach
61% did not respond
28% responded

Number of Responses: Fortune 100 Companies

These three responses—from Massachusetts Mutual Life Insurance, Amazon.com, and Walgreens—were the worst experience for me as a journalist. I can understand the 61 companies that chose not to respond at all, but to send an automated email promising a response and then not to deliver is just lame. I wonder if these companies' communications mottos are "Overpromise and underdeliver"?

Three responses—from DuPont, Sysco, and FedEx—were so moronic I had to laugh:

DuPont: *DuPont Policy requires that all survey requests be submitted in writing or faxed to the following: DuPont Company, Survey Response, [address]. When your survey arrives, it will be screened and routed to the most appropriate resource within DuPont for review and response; however, DuPont does not commit to respond.* (First of all, what survey? However, I did do what they asked, sending my request in writing. I have not received a response. But to be fair, DuPont said that the company does not commit to respond.)

Sysco: *Your comment has been submitted to our Website Feedback department. Thank you for your interest.* (Huh? "Website Feedback department?" I didn't get a response.)

FedEx: Although FedEx pioneered overnight package delivery, I guess they don't care about real-time delivery online. Nor do they read their emails carefully; 20 days after I sent my request, I received this: *Thank you for your inquiry. I regret we are unable to address your concerns via this avenue. We regret that FedEx does not have the resources to respond to student questions individually. However, there is a wealth of information on the FedEx website.* (Hey FedEx: STUDENT questions? Did you even bother to read my email or check my credentials? Be sure to tell your CEO, "UPS runs rings around us in real time.")

How Fast Does the *Fortune* 100 Respond?

Question my methodology all you like. Okay, so I'm not Thomas Friedman of the *New York Times*. And I'm not a statistician. But I write for a bunch of publications with many readers. And I'm the author of a global bestseller in a category that should cause PR people to sit up. I write about marketing and PR, for Pete's sake!

So if I can't find a way to contact your company's media-relations team, and I can't get an intelligent response from them—or any response at all—I don't

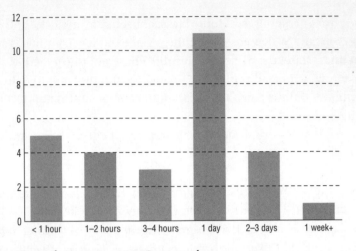

Response Speed: *Fortune* 100 Companies

think it's a stretch to say something is badly out of whack in your real-time communications infrastructure.

Why is it that only a quarter of the *Fortune* 100 companies respond in real time to media inquiries? The fastest were the five companies that responded in less than one hour. Twelve of the companies responded the same day I sent the inquiry, and another 11 responded the next day.

These companies that have developed a real-time mind-set are leaders in more ways than one. A comparison of 2010 stock prices reveals that on average the publicly traded Fortune 100 companies that responded to my inquiry (those engaged in real-time communications) beat the S&P 500 stock index, while the others on average underperformed the index. During the period—closing price on December 31, 2009 through closing price on September 3, 2010 (when this book went to print)—the stock prices of 65 percent of companies that responded were up, while only 39 percent of those that did not respond were up. For detailed analysis, please visit www.davidmeermanscott.com/documents/Real_Time.pdf.

This research confirms what I've suspected all along. Even the biggest companies can respond in real time if they put their minds to it. I've seen the leaders. I can name names.

Unfortunately, this research also confirms my fear. Three-quarters of the *Fortune* 100 either couldn't be contacted or failed to reply. (See the appendix for how each company fared.) That's not good enough in today's always-on world. If you own shares in one of these companies, you might want to write the CEO and ask why. Then again, you may not get a reply.

6 Engage the Media at Their Convenience

It was late, and I was ready to call it a day. I thought I'd check email and voice mail one last time before leaving my little office and heading home. The message, from a reporter at *BusinessWeek,* was short and to the point: "I would like to speak with you about a story I'm doing on Web marketing. Please call as soon as you can."

I knew I should call right away. But it had been a busy week and I was tired. I had a nagging feeling in my gut as I shut my door without having phoned the journalist. I could have called on my mobile driving home (safely, of course, with a headset) or after dinner with my family. Normally I respond to reporters immediately. It's what I do. I don't know what the heck I was thinking.

I called first thing next morning instead.

"I've got everything I need," the *BusinessWeek* reporter said. "Thanks anyway."

Later on that nagging feeling in my gut returned as I read the reporter's story online. It was great. A story in one of the world's premier business publications about a subject I know a great deal about. It was a story *without* a quote from me. I could see exactly where my remarks would have been inserted in the text. Instead of my thoughts, there was a juicy quote from someone else.

Damn, I felt foolish.

For days I kicked myself every time I thought about the real-time opportunity I'd squandered. By choosing to return the reporter's call on *my* time (not *his*) I was left out of the picture. My voice was not heard.

Always On

What was once a predictable 24-hour news cycle driven by the evening TV news and newspaper print deadlines is now an always-on, real-time, constantly evolving flow of news from thousands of mainstream sources backed by feeds from millions of citizen journalists via blogs, Twitter, YouTube, Flickr, and the like.

As you have read in earlier chapters, it started in finance as real-time information providers like Bloomberg, Dow Jones, and Reuters transformed the markets from a cozy old-boys' network to a global network that instantaneously informs billions of dollars in trading activity. Years later, as political and celebrity news went real time, upstarts like Politico and TMZ grew quickly as older, slower media titans contracted or closed.

Today, the mainstream media are feeling the same force of change. Having adapted, some media outlets are thriving. But many more are withering away because they cling to the old paradigm. Smart editors and reporters update blogs and media web sites in seconds. Consumers post videos and photos on the Web anytime where the media can see them. Reporters now rely on Twitter for instantaneous leads from citizen journalists—who are often reporting from the scene as events unfold.

The Revolution, Live on YouTube and Twitter

On June 12, 2009, election day in Iran, incumbent Mahmoud Ahmadinejad was declared the winner over three challengers. Protesters immediately took to the streets, launching what many were calling a "revolution." Given Iran's strained relations with the West, few foreign reporters were there to cover it. But that didn't stop the world from getting the news in real time. Ordinary Iranians risked their lives to film and post video and photos of the protests on YouTube and Flickr. People on the scene provided running commentary on Twitter. As a result, the world's media were able to run amazing photos and video from the streets of Tehran—including heartbreaking footage of an innocent young woman being killed by security forces.

Even though the mainstream media wasn't there, the world still received text, sound, and images in real time.

> The media is already operating in real time. You must, too.

We have all witnessed the media revolution that has brought us vast amounts of information at lightning speed. What has been largely over-looked, though, is the failure of most businesses to adapt to today's real-time news environment.

Get in Sync with the Real-Time News Cycle

For companies seeking media coverage, the conventional method relies on the PR team to spend a week drafting a press release that is then vetted by management and legal counsel. Weeks later, once the release finally gets distributed, PR staffers work the phones to plead with journalists to write about it.

When a company is thrust into the spotlight by a fast-breaking news situation, it works the opposite way. Reporters phone the company, urgently pleading for updates or comments. In this case, the PR staffers are forced to stall for time as they consult with management, PR agencies, and lawyers.

At least under the old rules everyone knew the timetable. You had until late afternoon to make a statement in time for the evening newscast and tomorrow's paper. Today, that just won't wash. If you don't react in real time the story will move on without you.

When a new corporate crisis erupts we often get fresh evidence that yet another business still doesn't understand real-time communications. During the critical hours as the story breaks the company is silent as senior executives huddle in endless meetings with the corporate communications team, the PR agency, and the lawyers. Even worse, local PR staffers twiddle their thumbs waiting for head office on the other side of world to wake up and authorize a statement. Is it morning in Toyota City yet?

Whatever value there was to gain from crafting a carefully calibrated response is all-too-often negated by initial silence that makes the company look like it has something to hide. And often as not, when it finally arrives, the cautious, committee-drafted response comes out sounding like gobbledy-gook-laden weasel-words.

Today, it is imperative to respond to the media when they need you.

Senior management should be aware of what the world is saying about the company in real time—in both mainstream and social media. When the company comes under the spotlight, management and the PR team should be ready to react within the hour.

> The best time to influence a news story is *Now*—as it is breaking.

The Old Media Relations Timeline

Here's an extreme—if hypothetical—example of how many companies get it wrong.

Imagine a story has appeared in an influential trade magazine about product deficiencies in the new release by Company X. Here's how many old-style companies might react:

Day 1: As the magazine comes out, senior management is informed that this story may have negative consequences for the company. A task force is convened to deal with the issue, including representatives from PR, legal, the product group concerned, and the PR agency.

Day 2: Task force members meet in the morning and then spend the rest of the day conducting research and formulating recommendations for response.

Day 3: The task force meets with executives to go over what happened, present recommended actions, and make a decision about what to do.

Day 4: The task force verifies facts, reviews final plans, prepares to execute the planned response, and creates needed materials (such as a press release).

Day 5: The company posts the response on a web site, issues the press release, and preps executives who will be made available for media interviews.

That's *one week* gone right there. In the real-time media world, a week is the same as a century. The moment is lost. You've completely blown it! #Fail.

Amazon.com as Big Brother

Now let's look at a real example of way-too-slow media relations—from a company that ought to know better. This is how Amazon.com missed a chance to quickly clear up negative reports about one of its products and assure customers that it cares.

In the summer of 2009, a publisher offered books for sale through the Amazon.com Kindle e-book reader. But it did not own the copyright for these titles that included George Orwell's *1984* and *Animal Farm* (more on the delicious irony later).

Having discovered this lapse, Amazon.com removed the unauthorized works from customers' Kindle accounts on July 16, without any notice as to why they were doing so. At the same time, Amazon.com refunded the money customers had paid for them.

Kindle users were annoyed to find these e-books had just disappeared. Poof! Products purchased from Amazon.com were no longer in their possession.

The Kindle community reacted swiftly, with hundreds of people commenting in the Kindle forums on the Amazon.com community *on that very first day*. Here is an example of one angry customer post to the Kindle forum:

This happened to me too. What ticked me off is that I got a refund out of the blue and my book just disappeared out of my archive. I emailed Amazon for an answer as to what was going on and they said there was a 'problem' with the book, nothing more specific. I'm sorry, when you delete my private property - refund or not - without my permission, I expect a better explanation than that. And, BTW - Pirated books showing up on Amazon-not MY problem- hire more people to check them BEFORE you sell them to me. I call BS on the 'sometimes publishers pull their titles' lame excuse someone else got too.

In addition to posting to the Kindle forums on Amazon.com, many people tweeted and blogged their ire. Negative sentiment gained steam quickly, in part because many Kindle owners are also savvy social media users and active on Twitter. Amazon.com should have known this community would react swiftly.

Over the next week, many mainstream media outlets ran stories. For example, the July 18, 2009, *New York Times* lede went like this: "In *1984*, government censors erase all traces of news articles embarrassing to Big Brother by sending them down an incineration chute called the 'memory hole.'"

Ouch! Irony! Amazon.com as Big Brother removes George Orwell's *1984*. But as more and more media picked up the story there was *no official comment* from Amazon.com. This further angered customers.

Finally on July 23, a week after the story broke, Amazon.com CEO Jeff Bezos finally apologized in a statement on the Amazon.com Kindle customer community forum.

> This is an apology for the way we previously handled illegally sold copies of *1984* and other novels on Kindle. Our "solution" to the problem was stupid, thoughtless, and painfully out of line with our principles. It is wholly self-inflicted, and we deserve the criticism we've received. We will use the scar tissue from this painful mistake to help make better decisions going forward, ones that match our mission.
>
> With deep apology to our customers,
>
> Jeff Bezos
>
> Founder & CEO
>
> Amazon.com

Immediately after Bezos's apology, the tone on the Amazon.com Kindle forums changed dramatically. There were 13 comments *within the first 10 minutes*, most of them in support of Bezos. These included the following: "Thanks. It wasn't that big a deal to me anyway" (posted one minute after Bezos' apology); and "That took a lot of courage Mr. Bezos. Still a very loyal Amazon customer here.:)" (posted two minutes after the apology).

Yes, mistakes happen. Every organization is bound to face a similar situation sooner or later. However, in today's always-on world, companies must be prepared to respond as news happens. Initial issues are significantly compounded when a company does not react quickly. Silence over an entire week implies that a company either is totally out of touch or simply does not care.

In this example, the apology from Bezos was heartfelt and appropriate. But it came way too late. Clearly, with hundreds of people reacting in real time, Amazon.com should have been on top of the issue right away. They had a perfect opportunity to clear the air on Day 1, but they said nothing.

Imagine if, instead of waiting a week, Bezos had responded on July 16, the first day of customers' online reactions via the Kindle forums, Twitter, and blogs? I'd say things would have played out much differently. Had they apologized in real time, before the mainstream caught on, the story would have ended there.

Now let's take a look at what really goes on in a newsroom and how you can influence stories in real time, as they are being written.

Now: While News Is Happening

The *Wall Street Journal* (WSJ), published for more than 100 years, has the largest circulation of any newspaper in the United States. And thanks to its European and Asian editions, WSJ is now a global paper of record for business and finance. Thus, for public companies, positive coverage in the *Wall Street Journal* is as good as gold. So PR people covet it and do all they can to cultivate relationships with WSJ reporters.

Like many media properties, WSJ has gone through huge changes in recent years: Reporters now gather news online and publish stories on WSJ.com, the largest paid news subscription site on the Web, with nearly one million subscribers. Effectively, the *Wall Street Journal* has evolved into an electronic publishing powerhouse that happens to publish a daily newspaper.

In talking with WSJ reporters and editors, however, I was able to confirm my suspicion that most corporate PR teams still engage this news giant as if it were still no more than the printed morning newspaper their fathers read in the 1960s.

These people have yet to notice that many WSJ.com subscribers use email alerts and RSS feeds to get key news in real time via BlackBerry or the iPhone. WSJ content likewise appears instantly in trading rooms around the world.

Even in China and Japan, people get WSJ content in real time in their own languages. In fact, WSJ's Chinese feed is one of the fastest growing news sites in China.

What's more, WSJ content is now effectively distributed through social media because people point out stories to friends.

In an always-on world, people get news on their terms, from their platform of choice, and at the time convenient for them.

Just as delivery methods have changed, the way the news is *created* has been transformed as well. In the old days, when an editor was finished with a story, the text was simply sent to press along with the rest of tomorrow's edition. Today, with the click of one button the same story is sent to millions of people in an instant.

The *Wall Street Journal* of 2010 is not your father's newspaper.

Multiple Takes, One Story

Newspaper stories used to be carved in stone. Once the text had gone to print in the final edition nothing could be changed until the first edition the next day. Today, stories are updated in real time as new facts and mistakes are uncovered.

This creates great opportunity for observant, fast-reacting PR people. If a newspaper web site runs a story with inaccurate information on your company, call them on it instantly. If you can't get a retraction you can at least get your clarification added right away.

What's so cool about this is that once you know how the system works, you can influence stories as they are breaking. You can see your comments being used in real time on the newspaper's web site. And you can go to bed knowing that the print version delivered the next morning will more accurately reflect your side of the story.

> In the world of real-time media, no story is ever "finished." It can always be updated, corrected, followed up on, and added to.

Fixed or final deadlines are history. Today, as journalists craft stories and post updated versions online, you can influence the content throughout the process—if you're quick.

What this means is that PR teams can no longer hang around waiting for bosses or lawyers to sign off. The rules of engagement must give them authority to shoot on sight.

How They Make News in Real Time

For a look inside a real-time editorial operation, I spoke with Jon Gripton, senior news editor at Skynews.com, the online operation of Britain's first dedicated 24-hour TV news channel. Although best known as a TV station, Sky News is actually a "multi-platform provider," delivering real-time news online via Skynews.com, by radio via more than 300 commercial stations, on mobile phones, on iPhones, via SMS news alerts, and even on train platforms, Virgin Atlantic flights, and the ticker tape in Piccadilly Circus.

Gripton's team includes about 20 people during the 7 A.M. to 7 P.M. peak hours. But the newsroom is staffed 24/7, 365 days a year. And everyone contributes to the entire scope of news platforms.

"Sky News is a news channel that lives dangerously and doesn't believe in fixed bulletins," Gripton told me. "Nor do we believe the web site is the be all and end all. It's our shop window, if you like, but we're pushing our content out to everyone that'll have it."

Gripton says he and his team are constantly in the mix of what people are saying online. "We're not just talking with people, we're answering and taking part in the conversation, and that's why we were early in appointing a Twitter correspondent whose job is just simply to be there, to be Sky News's face on Twitter," he says. "It's a world where, more than ever, news travels by word of mouth, but also by fingers on a keyboard. All of the production staff, all of the reporters, and all of the web site producers are on Twitter, and we're all using TweetDeck." TweetDeck is a free Web application that lets you monitor multiple Twitter feeds, and multiple search terms, in real time.

"We're all on Facebook, and we're all using MSN Live Messenger, too," he adds. "You've just got to be plugged into these things and be part of it. We're about breaking stuff first, so all those ways of being alert to incoming material is what we're about."

Did You Hear the One about the Pornographic Robocall?

Contacting reporters as they write pays off for Shaun Dakin, founder and CEO of the National Political Do Not Contact Registry.

By feeding journalists interesting story leads in real time, Daikin and his organization have garnered attention in major outlets like *USA Today*, ABC News, and CNN.

The goal of Dakin's nonprofit organization is to get the word out that political robocalls (recorded phone messages from politicians and political groups) are exempt from the Federal Do Not Call Registry, which was established to allow U.S. consumers to opt out of telephone sales calls. It also maintains a database where U.S. citizens can register phone numbers to be added to the Political Do Not Call list.

Daikin monitors Twitter for words and phrases like "robocall" and, when appropriate, contacts people to learn about their frustrations. He gave me a typical example of how he does real-time media relations.

"About a month before the general election in 2008," Daikin told me, "at around 8 P.M. Pacific Time, I see on Twitter that somebody is getting a pornographic-like political robocall in Northern California. My antenna went up. I thought: 'This is interesting. Politicians typically don't do porno-like robocalls.' So I immediately responded to the two women [who were] having a conversation about this on Twitter, and I said, 'Hey, who was the candidate? Do you have the audio files? What were the specifics around this?' They responded back to me almost immediately, telling me who the candidate was."

It turns out that Zane Starkewolf, a Republican candidate for U.S. Congress in California's 1st District, sent robocall messages to 100,000 voters on October 26, about a week before the election.

The call featured a seductive female voice purring about Mike Thomson—Starkewolf's opponent—in the style of a phone sex worker. "Mike Thompson's been a baaad boy . . . we all said no to the bailout, but Thompson backed Bush, just like he did for the Patriot Act. [moan] Vote Yes for Zane."

Daikin used the content of the robocall to create a blog post in real time. Then he contacted the media right away. "I had a number of contacts in the Northern California media," he said. "Articles had already been written about what I was doing, in the *San Francisco Chronicle* and the *San Jose Mercury News*, and I'd been on TV and radio in the San Francisco area. So reporters knew who I was. I sent them an email and said: 'Hey, this guy running for Congress named Zane Starkewolf is doing this crazy, porno robocall.' By the next morning it was on all the local radio and TV news. And that evening, less than 24 hours later, it was on the Rachel Maddow show on MSNBC."

The local stories mentioned Daikin's National Political Do Not Contact Registry. Of course, any news about robocalls helps Daikin's organization, because it fuels the outrage many people feel about being interrupted at home by political announcements. The process of finding something interesting on Twitter, blogging about it, and contacting reporters all happened within minutes. And the payoff was a national story the next day. In this way, Daikin raises awareness about his organization. When CNN covers their activity, thousands more people sign onto the Registry.

How to Engage the Media in Real Time

When you're responsible for media relations at a larger organization or one that is frequently in the news, the advice from Jon Gripton at Sky News on how to engage is absolutely critical. But many people work for much smaller organizations that are not well known (like Shaun Daikin's nonprofit National Political Do Not Contact Registry). You may be like Daikin and see an opportunity to comment on something in the media even though your organization is not at the heart of a story. Are there ways for you to break through as well? You bet.

The primary tools of traditional media relations have included press releases, the telephone, and personal relationships with journalists. I'm not suggesting you forget the phone and the press release, but in the always-on online world you may find better ways to engage the media in real time.

Let's take a look at a number of ways to reach the media *right now*, when a story is breaking. Each of these techniques is powerful and effective, but when there is a fast-moving news story, it is difficult to predict which will work best. Sometimes the smart approach is multitiered—when you have something important to say, reach out in several different ways.

Knock on Doors the Media Have Created

Many mainstream media outlets have created simple ways for anybody to contribute to news stories. Some offer a dedicated email address or web site where news can be submitted. As more and more media outlets make use of photos, videos, and commentary from the public in their reporting, utilizing these applications is a great place to start to engage.

For example, the Sky News iPhone application—Britain's most popular news application—includes a button for submitting news. On the iPhone application, you just press a button and you can upload photos and video directly from your iPhone. Gathering news directly from the public, round the clock, is part of what makes Skynews.com's reporting so fast.

One of the best-known ways to publish news directly is through CNN iReport, where people take part in reporting the news and help shape what CNN covers. Steve Garfield, an independent video producer and author of *Get Seen: Online Video Secrets to Building Your Business*, has contributed to iReport a number of times.

"I was up in Maine for my niece's wedding, and Hurricane Kyle was hitting the Maine coast," Garfield says. "I took my MacBook Pro computer to the ocean, and I made a short video to show what the crashing waves were like. Then I drove to a local library that had free Wi-Fi and submitted it to CNN's iReport. A short while later, I was at brunch with the whole family and my cell phone rang. I was able to say to the family, 'Excuse me, it's CNN on the phone. Can I take this call?' which was fun. CNN wanted to make sure I took the original video because they wanted to broadcast it worldwide. That was pretty cool, and it was so easy."

Garfield also submits to New England Cable News through their Live Stream interface. He uses his cell phone to broadcast video live into the New England Cable News studio. "There was a big snowfall, so I went outside with the yardstick just to do what the weather people always do to show how much the snowfall is. I went live, and then the anchor in the studio said, 'Now we're going to go to Steve, and he's in Boston. And look at the snow that's out there.' I showed the snow at my house from my cell phone by broadcasting it live, and they put that on TV." Although both Garfield's examples are weather-related, the topic you submit could be anything that might interest reporters covering a story.

"Revolutionary" is an overused term these days—and I plead guilty. But it really is revolutionary that you can now upload video from your cell phone and get it broadcast in real time on a major TV network!

The point here is simple. If you want to reach the media, don't overlook the new doors media outlets have opened to make it easy for you to contribute news.

Use Hashtags in Your Twitter Messages

As we learned from Jon Gripton, reporters now rely on Twitter when reporting a breaking story. If you have something to say, and you want reporters to find it, tweet your thoughts. But to make sure that reporters do find it, be sure to use appropriate hashtags and IDs in your tweets.

A hashtag is a unique identifier that's used to mark something on Twitter. It is a single word (or acronym) preceded by the hash (sometimes called "pound") sign. For example, in late 2009 when Eurostar trains were stalled for hours in the Channel Tunnel, people used "#eurostar" as a unique identifier for any tweets related to the situation. A hashtag makes it simple for people to search Twitter and instantly locate all references to that particular subject, which are displayed in reverse chronological order (most recent tweet first). As journalists frequently search Twitter this way, they will get your message if you use hashtags. Within minutes, a reporter may contact you for more information.

David Curle is director and lead analyst at Outsell Inc., a research and advisory firm focused on the publishing and information industries. Curle uses Twitter in his research. "I use Twitter all the time as a filter and aggregator," he says. "When there's breaking news, Twitter search is absolutely my best tool. For example, a couple weeks ago, Google Scholar put up a database on U.S. case law—big news in the legal information world. I first found out about it through one of the Twitter feeds I follow, and then I went over to search Twitter for reaction from other Twitterers. Those tweets had lots of links to blog posts and other substantive information about the news. For those first few hours, there was *no* useful information about the event that didn't cross my regular Twitter feeds or the ones I found via search, so I felt I was really on top of it. Twitter has become a really important business tool for me to track breaking industry news."

Use Your Blog or Online Media Room to Get Your Voice Heard

When working on a fast-moving story, journalists often seek background information and quotes from experts' blogs or corporate online media rooms (special sections on web sites aimed at the media).

When you have something to say, it is a great idea to blog about it as fast as possible to get your ideas into the information mix. Colin Warwick, signal integrity product manager in the design & simulation software division of Agilent Technologies, uses his blog to get information out quickly. "Having a blog allows me to be spontaneous," he says. "For example, I can put diagrams up very quickly and let people know valuable information. If we needed to put content on the corporate site, it would take three days. With the blog, I can get into a conversation in just five minutes."

I've used this technique myself many times. For example, on Sunday, May 2, 2010, I was enjoying a cool glass of tap water while relaxing at home with my family. The phone rang. As I did not recognize what popped up on my caller ID, I let it go to voice mail.

The message was from my local community's "reverse 911" communications system that alerts everyone in town when there is an emergency. The message detailed a water main break in the area that had occurred several hours before. The problem necessitated boiling water before drinking.

I jumped online to learn more. At that point the news was incomplete. But over the next few hours, newspaper web sites started to report the story and TV stations began to show video of the massive leak. It was a real-time crisis communications effort for the state government, especially the Massachusetts Water Resources Authority (MWRA) because more than a million homes had water that was deemed unsafe to drink.

I was stunned at how well the situation was handled by local authorities, the City of Boston, the State of Massachusetts, and the MWRA. Throughout the day and into the night, Fred Laskey, executive director of the Massachusetts Water Resources Authority, was all over the news providing real-time updates. His information was detailed and he was always cautious about saying when things might return to normal.

I thought the authorities did an excellent job with the communications aspects of the situation. I blogged it the next day (while the crisis was still playing out) in a post titled "Massachusetts Water Resources Authority real-time crisis communications."

Less than two hours after I published the blog post, *Boston Globe* reporter Don Aucoin found it and contacted me for comment on a story he was in the process of researching and writing about the communications aspect of this emergency. He contacted me via email and asked if we could talk that day. I agreed and we were on the phone right away.

Aucoin's story *Long-honed alert system passes its test run* appeared on the front page of the *Boston Globe*. The story also ran online and was fed to the wire services for syndication. The story included a quote from me with a mention of my previous book *The New Rules of Marketing & PR*. But it was not the fact that I was an author that got me the quote. It was simply because I had a blog post related to a topic that Aucoin was working on and therefore I was an ideal person to speak with on the story. I posted early in the life of this breaking story and therefore was noticed by the journalist at the exact moment he needed me.

Bob Lutz, former vice chairman of General Motors, also used this technique on his *FastLane* blog, which he started way back in 2004. Lutz was early to blogging and frequently engaged journalists via his blog in real time. Before he retired, I spoke with him to learn more about his approach.

"I primarily use it as a method of getting our version of the truth out," Lutz told me. "We would get these press reports, which were blatantly off-base and factually incorrect. The old defense that you used to have with stuff like that is you'd have your communications guy call the editor and say, 'We want a correction.' And the correction either never came or it came on page 23 at the bottom, which is completely ineffective."

Lutz got detailed on his blog when he saw something in the news and wanted to respond right away. "I've enjoyed having my own voice. When I rebutted something—let's say the *Wall Street Journal* claims that the Chevrolet Cobalt is a disgrace because it's the only car in its class in the world with rear drum brakes—I was able to say, 'That's blatantly false. The following Japanese and German cars in that category all have rear drum brakes, and it's a perfectly acceptable braking system.' Well, okay, that doesn't interest millions of people, but I found that the *FastLane* blog was read by journalists. That was really my audience. If they saw that I was on top of what they wrote and was more than ready to rebut it in a heartbeat and make them look bad in front of their colleagues, it did make them much more cautious of what they wrote."

Your blog or company media room is a great place to add your take on a story as it is happening. But don't just write the post or edit the media room and walk away. Alert people to the information by tweeting about it or sending a link to the journalists who might be interested, together with your contact information in case they want to follow up with an interview request.

From the Podium

If you're someone who frequently speaks in public, sometimes a live event can be the perfect opportunity to add your take to a breaking news story.

This is particularly true of politicians who have reporters hanging on their every word. On September 15, 2008, Republican presidential candidate John McCain spoke at a Jacksonville, Florida, rally after several days of economic turmoil: "The fundamentals of the economy are strong," he said. Given great uncertainty in the markets on the day Lehman Brothers went bankrupt, the comment was seen by many as out of touch.

The Obama campaign quickly formulated a response to McCain's comments, which was delivered by Obama himself at a campaign event in Grand Junction, Colorado. "He doesn't get what's happening between the mountain in Sedona where he lives and the corridors of Washington where he works. . . . Why else would he say, today, of all days—just a few hours ago—that the fundamentals of the economy are still strong? Senator, what economy are you talking about?"

David Plouffe, campaign manager of Obama for America, writes about this real-time back and forth between the candidates in his book *The Audacity to Win: The Inside Story and Lessons of Barack Obama's Historic Victory*. Note how the immediate reaction is designed to get the Obama point of view to as many reporters as possible as quickly as possible, but also note the importance of having the first comment come from candidate Obama himself.

> Our response followed a standard formula. Insert a rebuttal to McCain's outrageous comment in Obama's next speech that day to create a back and forth, ensuring maximum coverage. Produce TV and radio ads for release by that afternoon and get them up in the states right away. Make sure all our volunteers and staff out in the states had talking points on this to drive home in their conversations with voters. Make sure all our surrogates campaigning for us, especially those doing TV interviews, relentlessly pushed the point. And make sure reporters understood that we thought this could be the defining moment of the campaign.

The same technique can be used in business settings. Consider how Apple Inc. ensures maximum press interest in new products by keeping them secret until Steve Jobs, Apple CEO, unveils them from the podium.

Send a Media Alert

A "media alert" is similar to a press release, but is intended to provide reporters with a specific bit of information as they are writing about a current topic.

Media alerts are usually posted on a company's online media room, but it is also important to send the alert through a press-release distribution service so it gets wide exposure. Press release distribution services are available in many countries and languages.

A Selection of the Larger U.S. News Release Distribution Services

- Business Wire: www.businesswire.com
- GlobeNewswire: www.globenewswire.com
- Marketwire: www.marketwire.com
- PrimeNewswire: www.primenewswire.com
- PR Newswire: www.prnewswire.com
- PRWeb: www.prweb.com

Media alerts are also used at large trade shows and industry events to alert media to news being made on the show floor. Here is an example of a media alert sent by Polycom, Inc., during the 2010 Consumer Electronics Show.

Media Alert: Polycom Demonstrates Its Cloud-Based Home Telepresence at 2010 CES

Who & What: At CES, Polycom, Inc. (NASDAQ: PLCM) will demonstrate a prototype of its home telepresence solution. In this demonstration, Polycom will bring its industry-leading, business-quality collaboration capabilities to the consumer market. Home telepresence will enable consumers to visit with friends and family across around the globe and seamlessly integrate with company video and telepresence networks, all from the comfort of home and in life-like, full-size 1080p HD. The demonstration will take place in IBM's meeting space which is designed to illustrate technologies for its "Smarter Home Enabled by Cloud Technology" vision.

When & Where: Come learn more about Polycom home telepresence as part of IBM's Smarter Home initiative:

— Interactive Live Demos: CES, Jan. 7–10, Las Vegas Convention Center, North Hall Upper Level, N227, N228 (by appointment only)
— ShowStoppers @CES: Jan. 7, 6–10 P.M., The Wynn, Lafitte Ballroom
— Smarter Home Panel Discussion: Jan. 8, 8:30–9:30 A.M., N227, N228

A media alert timed to a physical event such as the Consumer Electronics Show is designed to catch the interest of the hundreds of journalists who attend this massive show. In this case, Polycom hopes journalists will stop by for the demonstration or perhaps simply mention the new Polycom offering in their coverage of the show.

This media alert from Burberry is designed to reach both the media and consumers interested in fashion.

> Burberry will be live streaming its Burberry Prorsum Autumn Winter 2010 menswear show live from Milan
>
> Saturday at 6PM (Milan time) (GMT+1) at live.burberry.com
>
> Show viewers online will be able to comment on the show as it happens in real time directly on the site or through their Twitter or Facebook accounts.
>
> Viewers have been invited to watch the show live on Saturday in a video message from Christopher Bailey, Burberry Chief Creative Officer, recorded in Milan, where he is preparing for the upcoming show.
>
> This follows from the live streaming of the Burberry Prorsum Spring Summer 2010 womenswear show live from London, where Burberry was the first luxury fashion brand to allow viewers to comment online on the collection as it took pace.

Hold a News Conference with a Live-Streaming Video Feed

Another great way to get your information out there is to hold a live news conference with reporters and bloggers.

News conferences are a time-honored tool for politicians and major corporations that are covered by packs of reporters. For example, as they unveil new models at the annual Detroit motor show, automaker CEOs customarily address an audience of hundreds of reporters before taking questions from the floor. But what can you do if you're in Wichita, far from the media crowd?

Do a live-streaming video feed of your news conference so people who cannot be physically present can still see and hear what is being said in real time. There are several providers of live-streaming services, including Ustream.tv, which make it easy to set up a camera linked in real time to the Web. Some presenters now take questions from distant viewers, usually via Twitter or instant messaging platforms. It is also possible to archive the feed so people can watch later. Live-streaming news feeds are still rare, which surprises me because of the tremendous value of reaching additional reporters and bloggers.

For a look at an innovative way to do news conferences, I spoke with Mitch Germann, vice president of business communications for the Sacramento Kings professional basketball team. Germann also has responsibility for communications for the Arco Arena, where the Kings play.

"The majority of the press conferences that we have with the Kings are for basketball-related news," he says. "Last week we announced a contract extension for our president of basketball operations, and that was a press conference situation. Sometimes if you have a significant player retire, that's a press conference. After the draft, we have a press conference to introduce our new draft picks to the local media, and we have a media day prior to the start of training camp to let media come and talk to all the players and the coaches."

Germann also conducts occasional press conferences on the business side. "Prior to the 2009 to 2010 season, we worked closely with our mayor to form what we call the 'sellout committee' to try to sell out our first two home games," he says. "And so we used the mayor along with our owners to announce that initiative and announce the members of the committee."

The news conferences make it easy for local reporters who follow the team to cover important events. "There's the local daily paper, the *Sacramento Bee*, several weekly newspapers, along with four local TV stations, plus some local sports and news radio that cover us," Germann says. "If it's a business-related press conference, we also have the *Sacramento Business Journal*, which covers us more heavily on the business side."

The Sacramento Kings are one of the more progressive teams in the NBA when it comes to blogger access. "We have local fan blogs, which are very engaged, and we give them access and have credentialed them for games," Germann says. "So they attend press conferences as well."

The team streams live video from its news conferences when announcing significant news, allowing anybody to watch in real time—with no password protection. The press conference video archive is also available to bloggers and others so the content can be embedded for on-demand viewing.

One recent Kings Media Day attracted 12,005 views, including many sent via the Facebook/Ustream application, which allows fans to ask players questions in real time. By comparison, the event introducing the Kings' 2009 draft picks generated 10,482 views. These detailed measurements allowed

Germann and his colleagues to learn which events attract more viewers. From this the team has learned what days and times they can draw most viewers. "When we stream a press conference on a weekday at like 2 P.M.," Germann says, "we notice significantly more traffic compared to, say, Friday night at 7:30 P.M."

Germann also tracks mentions on Twitter and Facebook. He knows how many times people have retweeted, or linked to, or clicked on a link to a live-streaming press conference. But the value to the Sacramento Kings of providing live video of news conferences goes well beyond just viewership numbers.

"Technology is allowing fans to be closer to their favorite teams than ever before and giving them insight into things they've never previously seen," he says. "Live-streaming press conferences are a great way to pull back the curtain and give fans access to something that used to be a mystery and was only seen by the media. In the past, fans had to wait until they watched the local news to see highlights of a press conference, and even then it was only a brief recap with a couple sound bites—possibly skewed by the opinion of the reporter. Live-streamed press conferences give fans the opportunity to see the entire event in real time, form their own opinion, and help build a more direct relationship with the team."

With today's real-time news cycle comes both opportunities and risks. On the opportunity side, it is easier than ever to follow what's happening right now and insert your viewpoint into the mix. However, many people choose to avoid instant communications. They do not engage in real time. In a crisis (fire at a factory, the CEO arrested for fraud, a product defect that causes injury), any organization could be thrust into the news and need to comment in real time. In Chapter 7 we focus on real-time crisis communications techniques.

7 Crisis Communications and the Media

Sooner or later your organization should expect to face a crisis. And guess what? The news is likely to break outside normal business hours. Will you be ready to communicate in real time? Part of being prepared is knowing how mainstream media outlets put news together when a fast-breaking story is evolving. In Chapter 6 we learned how reporters put their stories together. In this chapter, we focus on working with the media when dealing with an issue that threatens to irreparably harm your brand. We also discuss how to communicate with your *customers* in a crisis in Chapter 10.

In Chapter 6, I told you about my discussions with Jon Gripton, the senior news editor at Skynews.com. As luck would have it, a crisis was unfolding in real time while I was speaking with him.

Eurostar and Silence

On the night of December 18, 2009, the Eurostar high-speed trains that link London with Paris and Brussels conked out deep inside the 50-kilometer Channel Tunnel. Hundreds of passengers were trapped in the tunnel and thousands of travelers were stranded on other trains approaching the tunnel and in London and Paris. But as hour after hour ticked by Eurostar said next to nothing about the cause of the breakdown, when trapped passengers would be rescued, or when service would resume.

The next day as I was speaking with him, Gripton and his team at Sky-news.com were racing to get the story in real time.

"Eurostar is in the middle of an absolute firestorm," Gripton told me. "They are showing how *not* to run public relations during a crisis. They're getting it so wrong, and Twitter is blasting them with hate."

For 14 hours the official Eurostar Twitter feed had been utterly silent. But as I checked out the Twitter stream, the public was lashing Eurostar at a rate of nearly one tweet a minute. Here's a sample of what I captured over a 10-minute period:

- "Euromoron—How long have these trains been running on a wing and a prayer, maintenance-wise??"
- "I am supposed to get #eurostar ski train on boxing day please please please may it be fixed soon!"
- "When Eurostar resumes ticket holders will be on a first come first serve basis to be on a train! This is unacceptable!"
- "If people power can change the outcome of UK's no1 single then getting rid of eurostars CEO should be easy"
- "i wonder why #eurostar doesnt have competition. virgin, kgv, ice please make routes to paris and ill never use eurostar again"

"It is really hard to get any information right now, whether you're a journalist or a traveler," Gripton said. "Eurostar PR is used to talking to business journalists about the intricacies of the company but not crisis public relations, and they're struggling. Today, they put out three messages saying trains are running this afternoon, then two hours later, oh no, we're wrong, sorry, trains not running at all, maybe tomorrow. It's a state of chaos."

In the absence of information from Eurostar, Gripton and his team were constantly filling the gap with posts about the crisis on the Skynews.com Twitter feed for breaking news (@skynewsbreak), which made them the most up-to-the-minute news source.

"We can see, based on who's coming to our sites and what they're searching for, that this has created a massive demand for information," Gripton said. "People are contacting us to say: 'Thank you so much for your Eurostar information because you were the only place we could get it.'"

Twitter as a Crisis Communications Tool ———

When things are moving fast and furiously, you've got to be available to the media. "If you're supposed to be the person who talks to the media," Gripton said, "then for God's sake, be available, and it doesn't matter if it's day or night."

So how do you make yourself available to Gripton and other journalists?

Like many journalists, Gripton is constantly available on Twitter, monitoring what's going on and seeing who has new information.

"For us it's 'we need it now,'" Gripton told me. "And as soon as you say it, we report it. So don't hide. Twitter is fantastic because I'm on there all the time. Just address the message to me and I'll see it."

That will work if you just want to contact Gripton. But to reach all journalists, and your customers, you need to use appropriate Twitter IDs in your tweets. In the Eurostar case, if someone had wanted to get the attention of both Eurostar and journalists covering the crisis, they could have put the Eurostar official Twitter ID (@little_break) into the tweet. Then, anytime people are searching for tweets by or about Eurostar using the Eurostar ID, they will see your tweet. Note that Twitter IDs are proceeded by the "@" sign to differentiate them from hashtags. Another way to catch the attention of particular media outlets or reporters is to reference *their* Twitter IDs in your tweets. For example, to say something to Sky News, you could have included the Sky News Twitter ID (@skynewsbreak) or even Jon Gripton's personal Twitter ID. Of course, none of this guarantees your tweet will be seen or that a reporter will follow up, but it's always worth a shot.

Here's an example that pulls all these ideas together. Had you been stranded on a Eurostar train during the crisis, you might have tweeted something like this: "I am stuck on #Eurostar & not moving for 3 hours. @little_break no help. @skynewsbreak I'm happy to talk."

Twitter's 140-character limitation means that a tweet frequently looks cryptic to the uninitiated. Translated, this says "I've been stuck on a Eurostar train for three hours (using the Eurostar hashtag ensures that people see your tweet in a search). The trains are not moving. The officials at Eurostar (who use the Twitter ID @little_break) are of no help to me. If the reporters at Sky News (who use the Twitter ID @skynewsbreak) want to interview me about this situation right now, please contact me."

Who knows? In a case like this, a reporter may well have responded asking for a phone number. The tweeter might have been interviewed live and heard worldwide. Or the reporter could have taken the chat private, using Twitter Direct Messages, and conducted an interview that way.

Real-Time Media Alerts

Many companies use media alerts to inform the public (via the media) in the wake of a natural disaster. (For more on media alerts, see Chapter 6.) For example, after a power failure an electrical utility might send a media alert to tell customers when power will be restored. Journalists simply cut, paste, and put it online.

CEOs sometimes issue short statements to indicate the company's position on an item of concern in the news. For example, the day Lehman went bankrupt the CEO of another bank might have used a media alert to calm fears about that bank's stability. Again, the purpose is to get a quote into the text journalists are writing and broadcasting as the story evolves in real time.

Connect with Journalists before You Need Them

Personal relationships are vital. Journalists tell me again and again that, when news breaks, they call people they already know, whose phone numbers and email addresses they have. They ask themselves, "Who might know?" then call straight away.

Obviously, the onset of a crisis is a tough time to introduce yourself properly, establish your credibility, and build a trusting relationship. Trying to go "off the record" on the first date is risky.

That's why you need to do it now. Reach out to reporters, analysts, and editors. Develop a rapport, so that when your expertise is suddenly relevant to a hot story in the news, they immediately think of contacting you. Here are a few things you can do today to build relationships with the media.

Follow the Publication and Its Journalists

If you regularly follow what individual journalists write or broadcast, you will understand their interests and attitudes.

Comment on Stories and Blog Posts

Many online publications give readers space to post comments on stories; and many reporters now blog. Use these channels to engage them. Like most people, reporters are susceptible to flattery, so praise their efforts (without going over the top). Better yet, feed them additional information relevant to what they're writing. If it's useful, the reporter will almost certainly note your area of expertise on the matter. That may lead to a one-on-one email discussion that allows you to build rapport.

If you write your own blog, you can also write a blog post that adds to a specific story, then link to it (using the names of both the reporter and the publication). Savvy reporters use Google alerts (or other services) to track every mention of their names and publications. Again, the reporter will learn about you. You'll become a known quantity, more likely to be called on to comment on a story as it breaks.

Send an Email Introduction

Then again, you can just knock on the door. Send a short, friendly email saying who you are and what you do. This is a good way to establish a relationship. Target a specific journalist. Be as simple and as short as you can, and in this introduction, do not pitch a story idea. For example, I might say: "I'm an expert in modern marketing and PR strategies." You can suggest the sorts of stories you can comment on. In my case, I could say something like: "I'm available to comment on stories about social media at the workplace, including Twitter, YouTube, and Facebook."

The more specific the better, because many reporters will file your information based on what you say you can comment on. (In my example, when news breaks about something related to Facebook in the workplace, I may get a call.) In your email, give full contact information, including phone numbers (work and mobile), your email, and IM addresses. If you have them, also include your blog or web site URL and Twitter ID.

Follow the Reporter on Twitter

Twitter is a great way to connect. Follow your favorite reporter, then use Twitter to build a relationship. Again, *give something first*, before expecting to receive. For example, you can point your followers to that reporter's work, using his or her Twitter ID in your tweet. I do this all the time. For instance, "Top startups to watch in 2010 from @ScottKirsner in Friday's Boston Globe http://bit.ly/7wwjF8." Note that because I used Kirsner's Twitter ID, he will see my tweet in his Twitter stream. This virtual "pat on the back" is an excellent way to start a relationship.

If they are on Twitter, you can usually find a reporter's ID at the beginning or end of a story. If not, use a search engine to find it. So if you didn't know Scott Kirsner's ID, a search for the word "Twitter" and "Scott Kirsner" would bring up his Twitter ID.

Never Spam Reporters

I've saved the most important advice in this section for last. Never, ever spam, pester, drone on endlessly, or otherwise annoy your journalistic contacts. If you provide information of value, you will be respected. If you are a pest, you will be ignored.

Thrust into the News When You Least Expect It

Sometimes, news breaks around you and puts you into a unique position to tell the story in real time. That's what happened to Netra Parikh on November 26, 2008, when terrorists staged a series of coordinated attacks in Mumbai, India (remembered by Indians as 26/11) that killed hundreds of people.

Visiting Mumbai, I spoke with Parikh about her horrific experience. She was on her laptop at home around 9 P.M. when she heard about the attacks from a friend. She immediately began tweeting on her @netra Twitter ID using the #Mumbai hashtag, alerting her followers to the mayhem in progress. She then started calling friends to confirm they had reached home safely, and asked each what they knew about the attacks in a dozen locations around the city. She also turned on the TV news, which was then reporting news of the violence.

"I started tweeting about the places where the shootings and bomb blasts were happening, and I started gathering news from whatever sources were available," Parikh told me.

Terrorists had stormed the city's iconic Taj Mahal Hotel and taken hundreds of people hostage. Viewers around the world watched the drama on live television. But police soon realized the terrorists were also watching TV news to learn what was happening outside the hotel. So authorities ordered a stop to live broadcasts from the Taj.

Once this conduit was cut off, Parikh suddenly found that her Twitter feed had become a key source for global media and local residents alike.

"I was able to get information from friends who at the time were living near the Taj Hotel," Parikh told me. "Then I started calling hospitals and counting the people admitted. That's how I learned hospitals required blood donations to aid the injured."

Parikh tweeted all the information she learned in real time, throughout the night of the 26th and over the two following days. Before it was all over, she had spent 60 hours straight at her keyboard, with no sleep.

"During 26/11 there were not many people in India tweeting and my feed became a kind of newsroom for international journalists," she said. "There was so much to do in order to use Twitter as tool of support and help for the victims. I was relaying information about the help lines of countries like the U.S., Brazil, Australia, and Sweden."

From the morning of November 27, Parikh was interviewed by journalists from all over the world. "I got my first call from CNN in the U.S. on the evening of the 27th, and then I got a call from CNN London at midnight." She was an important source for many journalists during the hostage drama and was quoted in Indian national newspapers, on CBS News in the United States, and other local news stations in the United States and Australia.

"Twitter becomes such a powerful tool in the time of crisis," she said, reflecting on her experience.

Today, Parikh is active raising money for victims through a site she started with friends: helpmumbai.pinstorm.com.

When You Have Hot News

There may come a time when you have important and unanticipated news to release. If you are sitting on an explosive story, then you are in control—at least initially. Your news may be positive, say a huge jump in sales or the announcement that your company is to be acquired by a larger, more famous competitor. Or the news may be negative.

Depending on the nature of the story, it's up to you to choose how you break it to the world. Your choices will greatly affect how the story spreads and how the public perceives you.

I firmly believe in telling the entire story up front along with all the data, photos, and video you can back it with. I also believe you should make spokespeople available day and night to explain the story. Even if the story is negative, if you tell it fully and transparently you will get credit for "fessing up." Do this and you can expect to be treated fairly. The worst thing is to look like you are hiding something. When you hide, people assume there is even more negative news coming. Hello BP!

In the face of bad news, the worst thing to say is "no comment." Some organizations try to bury the story by releasing it late on a Friday, over a weekend, during a holiday, or during a busy news day. That may work, but reporters will realize what you're doing and that will not help your credibility.

Conversely, when you have good news to tell, mornings and early in the week are usually best, because that's when journalists tend to be looking for stories to write. Slow news days are great because you know the media will have space to fill.

How to Deflate a Scandal

David Letterman, host of the highly popular *Late Show*, on NBC TV in the United States, startled viewers on October 1, 2009, by revealing someone had tried to blackmail him, threatening to expose extramarital affairs with his underlings.

I'll leave commentary about the tawdry aspects of this incident to the thousands of other people who weighed in with opinions on the sex angle. What impresses me is the skillful way Letterman chose to deal with the issue.

It is significant that the public first heard about the situation from Letterman himself. He delivered a deadpan description of the extortion attempt, and admitted that he had indeed had sexual relationships with women who worked for him. By doing this he immediately deflated the value of the threat to zero.

Letterman must have known the news would come out somehow. But facing up to that likelihood and *preemptively admitting it himself*, on his own terms in his own court (his top-rated television show), was a brilliant move nonetheless.

If bad news is going to come out anyway, it is better that you tell the story yourself and avoid looking like a deer caught in the headlights.

This story could have had all the elements necessary to fuel a scandal that might have been in the news for years: sex, celebrity, infidelity, greed, shame, lies, and more. But by getting to the bottom right away—admitting his sin— Letterman skillfully managed to deflate the scandal up front. As a result, much of the ensuing coverage focused on the venality of the blackmailer and not Letterman's indiscretions. Tiger Woods could have saved himself a world of pain had he taken advice from Letterman.

If you are facing bad news, the absolute worst thing to do—*konnichi-wa Toyota!*—is to let the media uncover a juicy new detail each day for months. Get to the bottom right away and put all the dirt on the table immediately. Tell the truth, apologize profusely, make amends, and move on—quick as you can.

The Time Is Now

As the media shed the 24-hour news cycle mentality in favor of continuous coverage, you need to keep pace. Be aware of what's happening around you. Engage reporters, analysts, editors, and bloggers as they craft their stories. Add to the mix by publishing your own story on your blog and online media room, or through media alerts and press conferences.

> You've got to train your mind to think in microbursts of immediate activity. When news is breaking, the time is now.

Let's close this chapter with a glimpse into how a media crisis was solved in real time at an organization that simply does not tolerate failure.

The Million-Dollar Door

First thing in the morning of July 21, 2009, Captain Nathan Broshear, director of public affairs for the United States 12th Air Force/Air Forces Southern, got a real-time media-relations shock. The *Drudge Report* had just posted a story about a "million-dollar door" at Dyess Air Force Base in Abilene—deep in the heart of both Texas and Broshear's bailiwick.

The story resulted from an obscure report on the Recovery.gov web site that described how $1.4 million in government funds were being allocated to AFCO Tech to "fix a door" at the base.

The media smelled a juicy scandal. After all, a door is a door and how much could that reasonably cost? The news hook was easy to explain, easy to visualize, and short enough to fit into any medium: the Web, TV, or newspapers. Soon, the story was being reported by local Texas media and then nationally by FOX News's Glenn Beck, who said, "And in . . . Texas, Dyess Air Force Base is spending $1.4 million to repair a door at Building 5112. Wow, what happened to that door? That's a lot of repairing, you know. Can we buy a new one, and cheaper?"

Broshear did some quick research and found that the "door" was actually a six-panel, 150-foot wide hangar door used to protect Air Force B-1 Lancer bombers worth $250 million each. The door includes automatic electrical drive mechanisms and highly secure safety devices, and it is hurricane and tornado proof. In addition, the $1.4 million contract included repairs to the hangar building itself.

Broshear knew he had to respond—*right now*. "We sent base photographers out to the hangar to take photos from every possible angle," he told me. "They also took photos with a man standing next to the door and a pickup truck parked just a few feet in front of the building, so people could get a sense of scale. We then drafted a short email to Matt Drudge and attached the photos."

Because Broshear's commander started to hear about the "million-dollar door" from his contacts, Broshear knew that the story was moving swiftly in military circles as well as in the media. He knew he had to do more. Immediate action was required to stop the spread of the inaccurate story.

"To keep on task, I kept asking my team, 'How many links to this site are going up right now?'" Broshear told me. "'How many blogs, other news sites, or email forwards containing this story are going out *right now*?'"

His team quickly added the photos and information about the door contract to the media section of the 12th Air Force web site and also sent the information to the Air Force press desk for distribution to the Pentagon press pool. This quick action extinguished the potential story among the military press corps.

"Most hadn't heard the initial, incorrect version when they got the email and photos," Broshear says. "Since these reporters have all been to military bases, they understood the size of the building in question and the costs associated with those types of large hangars, so nobody covered the story."

Quick work by Broshear and his team over a short period of time squashed what could have exploded into a huge story. What a headline! A million-dollar door, bought with your tax dollars! But there was much more to the story, and telling the Air Force's side was essential in those early minutes. "A timely response was required," he says. "We had to tell our side of the story with a short, simple response coupled with self-explanatory photos illustrating how the 'million-dollar door' headline was misleading. This ensured the story lasted only a matter of hours."

The speed at which stories like this break is much faster today than it was even a few years ago. "In the past, you could work a story in the morning for a noon broadcast, or work with a reporter until four so they could be ready for the evening show," Broshear says. "Today, we must be able to respond within minutes to any report. Even hours are too long. In the time it took to get the photos and draft the email, news outlets from all over Texas, Washington, and New York were already calling for comment. Several media outlets planned to report the story without confirmation, but all later dropped stories after getting the facts. I've seen a simple headline launch congressional investigations, stop projects, and even end careers. You have to be ready to respond to any outlet quickly, clearly, and directly."

When news breaks and you've got something to say, there is no precise formula to follow. Actually, I think that's good, because it means those of us who think in real time and understand that we need to move *now* will maintain a huge advantage over those slow plodders who insist on checking, planning, and calling in the lawyers.

If the stinky stuff ever hits your fan, I wish you luck and hope this chapter has helped you prepare.

8 What Are People Saying about You *This Instant?*

"**W**ho the Hell ARE these People?" was the heading I put on a blog post in late 2009. In it, I showed a stock photograph and asked my readers: *Who are these young, happy, pretty, multicultural people with great teeth and even better hair who hang out with notebook computers in sleek and modern conference rooms on B2B company web sites all over the world? Who are these international inhabitants of virtual corporate locales?*

I went on to describe the stock images that adorn many corporate web sites: *The problem with the "B2B happy multicultural conference room with computer shot" is that it has become a cliché. This kind of image is so overused it has become meaningless. These models don't look like you. They don't look like your employees. And they don't look like your customers (unless you run a modeling agency). Because these models don't look like you or your customers, it is insulting and demeaning to everyone (your employees and customers especially) to use these shots on your homepage and throughout your site.* After posting the piece, I also tweeted "Who the Hell ARE these People?" with a link to it.

Who the Hell ARE These People?

The reaction was immediate. The first retweet (when someone forwarded my tweet to their followers) came within seconds. Soon many people were tweeting and retweeting, pointing their followers to my post. The first hour averaged one tweet every two minutes. Additional tweets throughout the day

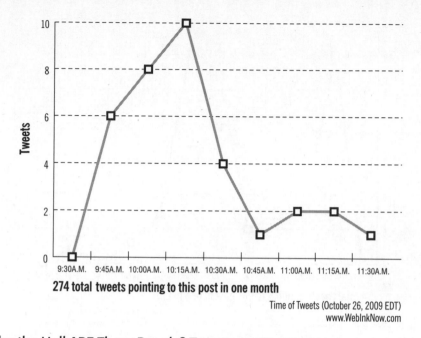

274 total tweets pointing to this post in one month

Time of Tweets (October 26, 2009 EDT)
www.WebInkNow.com

Who the Hell ARE These People? Tweets per Quarter Hour

drove many thousands of people to the post. Here's a graph of what the first two hours of tweets looked like. Notice the bell-shaped curve typical of the law of normal distribution, as outlined in Chapter 3.

After the initial flurry of activity, at 2:46 that afternoon Chris Brogan tweeted: "Thanks to @dmscott for making me laugh out loud. Who the hell ARE these people?" Because Chris is extremely popular on Twitter (with more than 100,000 followers at the time), many more people were exposed to my blog post, and many more people tweeted it. The next graph, providing data for the first 12 hours after I released the post, shows two distinct bell-shaped curves (one from my initial tweet and one following Chris Brogan's tweet). In the graph, you can see the power generated when one person with many followers points to something. Chris doubled the number of people exposed to my blog post. Also notice the small bump of interest at the end of the day. I traced this result to my followers in Australia and New Zealand, who because of the time difference were "offline" when the action peaked. When they saw the post in the morning, a few of them tweeted, too.

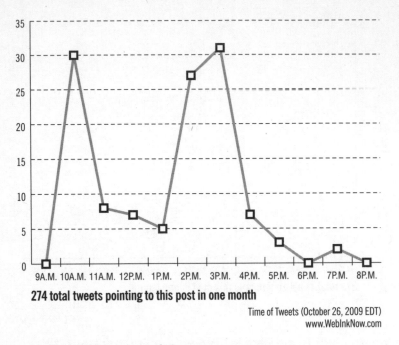

274 total tweets pointing to this post in one month

Time of Tweets (October 26, 2009 EDT)
www.WebInkNow.com

Who the Hell ARE These People? Tweets per Hour

At the same time, people also started to leave comments on my blog, a dozen in the first hour and 30 more throughout the first day. What intrigued me, though, is how quickly interest in the post trailed off.

In studying trends of online conversation, I've found that interest almost always follows the same pattern and tapering off at about the same speed. Take a look at the next graph which shows the number of blog comments per day. You'll see how the number follows the predictable power law pattern as the blog post becomes "old news."

The speed with which an item loses people's interest on Twitter is even more dramatic. The next graph clearly shows the Real-Time Marketing & PR Power Law trail-off pattern (introduced in Chapter 3). I dug into the data in some detail. The first day's tweets were primarily retweets. In other words, the majority of people who tweeted found out about my blog post from other Twitter users. They saw a tweet from me or from Chris Brogan or someone else and then visited my blog to read the post. Some people who found the post interesting then chose to use Twitter to alert their followers by simply retweeting—the Twitter equivalent of forwarding an email. This flurry of real-time retweets (more than 100) was mostly over by the end of the first day.

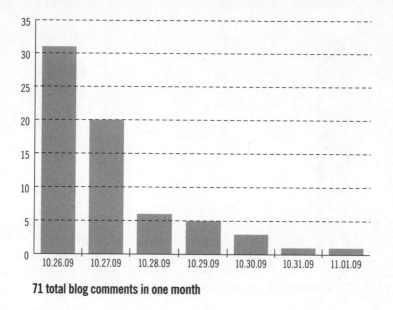

71 total blog comments in one month

Who the Hell ARE These People? Blog Comments per Day

The next several days' tweets, however, were original (not retweets)—and the reason is simple. Many of my blog followers learned of my post through their RSS readers (RSS stands for "really simple syndication," which lets you subscribe to blogs, receiving updates as they are posted) or through Feed-Blitz (which delivers posts via email in a daily batch). So many did not see my post until two days later, and their retweets generated a second wave of interest.

You can also see a small spike in tweets on October 31. In honor of the scariest holiday Americans celebrate I had tweeted this: "Some creepy and scary corporate photos especially good for Halloween!" That led to a dozen or so retweets and several hundred more views of the original post.

Why am I spending so much time analyzing one little blog post? Because it illustrates perfectly how online popularity works. A real-time phenomenon occurs as people jump into an active discussion like the one I started about stock photography.

The really dynamic conversation only happens on the first day or in the first few hours following the Real-Time Marketing & PR Power Law. It works like this. As people read fresh content on blogs or mainstream news sites, they will often leave a comment. And since the earliest comments typically

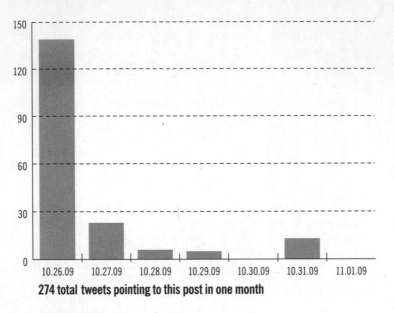

274 total tweets pointing to this post in one month

Who the Hell ARE These People? Tweets per Day

appear first in the list, those who get the first word in the conversation are most widely read. Their voices stand out in the ensuing chatter.

With my stock photo post, the first several comments were read by nearly 10,000 people while the last few were read by a few hundred at best. Again, this pattern illustrates the importance of speed in all aspects of doing business online. When you speak out quickly, people hear your ideas.

> Reaction speed is critical. Of course, you can't react unless you instantly know (and understand!) what's being said.

In this chapter, we look at a wide variety of tools you can use to monitor what's being said online. But unlike Chapter 7, where we focused on monitoring the mainstream media and bloggers, here we look at how you can listen to ordinary people—to your customers as they talk about your company.

Some of these services are free and simple to use, while others are sophisticated applications used by big business and governments. Big or small, it doesn't matter: You need to know what's being said about you and about the issues critical to your business. And in order to react in real time, you need to know quickly.

Tracking Those You Know

The first priority is to listen to bloggers, analysts, journalists, and others who talk frequently about you and your business. Start by identifying as many voices as you can. List all the relevant trade journals. Find securities analysts who cover your sector. Look overseas to find content on your industry in distant markets. Search for relevant online forums or chat rooms. Pinpoint bloggers who have opined on issues relating to your business. Keep searching continuously for new sources.

To find these voices, start by checking the search engines (Google, Yahoo!, Bing, and so on) for all the relevant keywords and phrases you can think of: your company, customers, competitors, prospects, product categories, buzzwords—whatever you can think of.

Use specialized blog search engines like Google Blog Search, IceRocket, and Technorati to find bloggers interested in subjects related to your business.

Once you have identified key sources, the next step is to begin monitoring what they say in real time. As its name suggests, the really simple way to do this is using RSS, "really simple syndication"—a tool that allows you to harvest content from hundreds of blogs and news feeds without having to visit each one. RSS feeds update each time a site changes, alerting you to relevant information on topics that you specify. I use Google Reader for this, but there are many RSS readers to choose from.

Twitter, as mentioned, is a great way to stay on top of breaking news. Many bloggers, journalists, and media outlets now use Twitter to drive traffic to fresh content as it appears. If these sources are active on Twitter, you'll find a Twitter ID on their sites or blogs. Use TweetDeck or another Twitter-monitoring tool to aggregate your important Twitter feeds (that is, sets of tweets important for your business) so you can easily monitor what's being said by the people who matter to you.

The goal here is to know what people say *immediately*, so you can comment in real time if appropriate. And that is certainly easier when you have already identified people likely to talk about you.

It's like joining a circle of your friends at a cocktail party: You can anticipate their conversations will interest you. And because you are accepted by the circle you can easily jump in with your own thoughts.

So as you monitor the people who talk about you, it is good to get a sense of what each person's interests are. If someone writes about your industry, get to know their specific interests. Comment occasionally on their posts or articles even if they don't refer to your company or products. If you're already a known voice, your opinion will be taken more seriously when you jump in to discuss something directly related to your business.

The benefit of reacting quickly and being among the first to comment is huge. You are seen as someone who cares and is on top of what's going on.

It is equally important to let people who write about you see that you're paying attention. Even to those who write negatively about you, respond politely and without anger. This can build positive rapport to help ensure that next time they will try to get the facts straight and perhaps even ask you to confirm information before they publish. What's more, you can anticipate they will be more polite. Having received your polite, friendly messages they will think twice before flaming you!

Choosing to Respond (Or Not)

In the course of monitoring your regular sources, you may come across people discussing your company. So how do you decide who gets a response and who gets ignored? There is no easy answer to this. Some people are just plain crazy, and you don't want to get dragged into dialogue with a psycho.

I like the way Christopher Barger, director of social media at General Motors, decides. Barger says what's important is to figure out who is *thoughtful*: "If they are critics or if they're supporters, it's who is really thoughtful and who is just lobbing bombs or seems to be throwing softballs at you," he told me. "It's great to have supporters, and you're always going to have critics who can't stand you no matter what you do. If someone raises a thoughtful criticism and people answer back with thoughtful responses, we can tell it's an intelligent conversation, and one we ought to get into."

Barger says this "thoughtfulness" rule of engagement surprises many people, who assume that the sheer number of people reading is the most important factor. "You have to throw the old concept of numbers away," he says. "One school of thought says, 'This person has 200,000 followers on Twitter or a blog that millions of people read, so we've got to go in there.' But you can have just as much impact engaging with someone who has [fewer] followers if that person [is influential]."

Listening in to Millions of Discussions in Real Time

So far we've talked about interacting in real time with people you have identified as important centers of influence. But what about the millions of people out there you don't yet know? If you have a sizable business there are bound to be people out there talking about you on social media who aren't on your radar. The good news is that you can still monitor the millions of conversations happening online and instantly respond to both opportunities and threats.

A decade ago, when I was vice president of marketing and public relations for a NASDAQ-traded business-to-business technology company, we measured our PR programs with a "PR clip book." Each month, our PR agency would send over a bound copy of the book, including all the latest news articles and broadcast transcripts that mentioned the company. Although this was a great tool for justifying our existence to the bosses—"just look at all these"—it was a terrible way to stay on top of our reputation in real time. The information was so damn old by the time it reached us, we could never react and engage effectively!

Fast-forward to 2010. Now everyone—not only B2B companies but also consumer brands, consultants, nonprofits, and even rock bands, churches, and colleges—has a tremendous opportunity to reach people and engage them in real time.

Today's online tools offer instant knowledge of what's being said about you and your activities. This awareness allows you to engage as discussion unfolds rather than be caught offside weeks later when a clip book lands on the boss's desk.

For individuals and smaller outfits, the free (but powerful) applications available online are sufficient to monitor news and conversations relevant to your activities. I've got a list of useful tools here.

Large enterprises, on the other hand, generate so much discussion that it is usually worth investing in a more sophisticated social media analytics service. This is particularly true for consumer brands, government agencies, well-known nonprofits, and large-scale political campaigns. We'll look at some of the premium services later in this chapter.

How to Stay on Top of the Millions of Discussions Going on Right Now

- Create a comprehensive list of search terms relevant to your activities. Include the names of your company, senior executives, competitors, customers, prospects, products; plus any relevant buzzwords or phrases— every term you can think of!
- Use search engines (e.g., Google News or Yahoo! News) to set up a news alert using those search terms. This will automatically inform you in real time when any of your search terms crop up. Set up alerts on blog search engines, too. Note that if you choose Google Alerts, you can set the alert to let you know when a phrase appears in multiple content types, so one set of alerts can help you monitor blogs, newsfeeds, web sites, and more.
- As monitoring progresses you will likely need to modify your search terms as some yield a flood of "false hits" and others nothing. Some services offer advanced features that allow you to refine your searches. For instance, Boolean operators like "and," "but," and "not" can make your searches more specific. If you need help, look for independent consultants with a background in library science. Add new search terms as you go along (watch for tags authors apply to items that interest you). It's an ongoing process, so you can't just set your search terms and forget about them.
- Monitor your search terms on Twitter, too. Some tweets will show up in your news alerts if you use a service that indexes Twitter, like Google. Even so, I find it's more effective to monitor Twitter directly. Use a Twitter monitoring tool like TweetDeck or HootSuite to catch your key phrases. You can also use Twitter's own search function for one-off searches.

A $250-Grand Tweet!

Some people argue that only major consumer brands need to monitor what's said about them online. Not true! Smaller outfits and business-to-business companies might generate less traffic, but that makes it all the more crucial to know what's being said.

Take the example of Avaya Inc., and their specialist telecommunications technology used in call centers. Avaya watches carefully what's being said on social networking sites to win and keep customers.

When Paul Dunay joined Avaya as global managing director of services and social marketing in 2009, he quickly set to work building the company's social media profile, including its Twitter presence. An important aspect of his strategy focused on how Avaya could better understand and respond to what others said about the company.

"Listening to the market and engaging in the right conversations enables Avaya to quickly spot issues and opportunities as they arise, even before anyone contacts the company," Dunay told me.

Avaya established a presence in four key social-media realms: blogging, forums, Facebook, and Twitter. Twitter assumed a key role as a company listening post and early response center, both for resolving issues and creating opportunities to engage potential customers.

Initially, Dunay monitored all Avaya Twitter mentions and other social media traffic himself, forwarding tweets and posts that required a response to a qualified support or sales representative. When it became clear that the number of mentions was too many to watch on his own, Dunay secured official backing from Avaya's chief marketing officer to build a cross-functional, global team.

Dunay organized an initial team comprising seven Avaya social-media early adopters, a team that has since grown to include 50 members. "Team members from marketing, support, legal, and other business units monitor 1,000 to 2,500 company mentions and discussions each week using Tweet-Deck, with Radian6 [a social-media monitoring and analytics tool] providing backup to capture missed items," he says. "A team member who 'hears' about an issue requiring further action posts it on an internal wiki. Responses are not automated. Instead, the issue is assigned to someone with the knowledge and authority to handle it."

Dunay says issues addressed with customers through social networking sites include product support, parts availability, financing and billing questions, and product end-of-life issues, as well as support requests from channel partners. "Listening to and joining the Twitter conversations going on about Avaya enables the company to seize sales opportunities and generate revenue quickly, enhance support to channel partners, and address product and service issues before they have time to inflame," he says.

For example, the strategy delivered a quick payoff when somebody tweeted, "[Name of an Avaya competitor] or avaya? Time for a new phone system very soon." The tweet was spotted by Dunay's team in real time, and just minutes later they tweeted back using the @Avaya_Support Twitter ID: "@[Person's Twitter ID]—let me know if we can help you—we have some Strategic Consultants that can help you assess your needs." The individual who tweeted was indeed evaluating telephone systems right then and engaged with Avaya, resulting in a quick sale for $250,000. Less than two weeks later, the customer tweeted: "At [name of company] we have selected AVAYA as our new phone system. Excited by the technology and benefits to [name of company]." The customer was so happy with the Avaya services and the people at Avaya that he was working with that he tweeted again a few months later: "Getting ready to install our new avaya phone system—our customers will love it."

"A 57-character Tweet led to a $250,000 sale," Dunay says. "That's nearly $4,500 a character!"

Turning around a Critic

Sooner or later, anyone who monitors what people say in real time will come across an upset customer who has nothing but bad things to say about the company and its products. It's great when this happens!

That may sound counterintuitive, but occasions like this present real-time engagement teams with great opportunities to deliver value.

When people vent their frustrations on social media, they just don't expect a response from the company. Consumers assume companies are too big or too preoccupied to care about engaging them. So the reason I'm bullish on negative expressions is that, when someone from *your* company engages in real time, it shocks the heck out of the complainer, frequently turning a critic into a supporter. I've seen it countless times. Complainers are happy that they've been heard, and frequently they tell others about the positive experience.

> Reacting intelligently and in real time to a critic shows that you are human and frequently gains you an advocate.

For example, my wife, Yukari Watanabe Scott (@YukariWatanabe), complained on Twitter (in Japanese): "Dear Amazon.co.jp, I take time to write reviews for Amazon.co.jp, but often they are not posted for more than a month, or only after I complain. I wonder if it's a good practice. I don't have the same experience with U.S. Amazon.com."

In *fewer than 10 minutes* came a real-time response from Hiroyoshi Watanabe (no relation to my wife), director and head of public policy Japan at Amazon Japan K.K. (@hiroyoshi): "I will have someone check the cause of the problem." My wife found this remarkable and told me about the experience. So here, as I pass the story on to you, Amazon gets positive PR.

The problem itself was fixed within 24 hours, and her reviews are now posted quickly to the Amazon Japan site. Amazon Japan turned a critic into a supporter with quick follow-up and a few well-placed, real-time words.

When You Don't Have an Immediate Answer

Instant response is the ideal in engaging the public in social media. When you jump into a discussion in real time, you delight the audience. And when the tone is negative, you can often turn it around, turning critics into advocates.

Of course, you won't always have a magic answer at hand. But jump in immediately nonetheless, identify yourself, sympathetically acknowledge the beef, and promise to find an answer. Simply *being there* in real time is what's important.

As with Yukari's Amazon Japan experience, there will be occasions where you personally don't have an immediate grasp of the issue. But given a day or even just a few minutes you can find one. Say so! Get a response out to let the person know you're on it, then go find the answer. But when you promise be sure to follow through. Remember that it's better to under-promise and over-deliver, so be sure to give yourself enough time. If you get the job done faster, so much the better!

"I don't think there is anything wrong with saying 'I don't know the answer to that right now, and it's going to take me a little while to track down the right person,'" GM's Barger says. "Now it would be a different story if I were saying, 'Well, I think I have an answer but I have to go run it past the lawyers.' That's a different thing; then you are being corporate and not being human. It's human to say, 'I don't have the answer right now' and I think that is acceptable."

Humanity, as Barger notes, is a critical element here. People don't expect a company representative to engage because we all experience so much nameless, faceless corporate neglect.

When was the last time you phoned a toll-free support line and *didn't get* sent into some sort of phone tree hell? People have come to expect that companies don't care. So when you actually respond to customers on social media in real time, they sit up and take notice. I've said it myself: "Holy cow! An actual human is listening to what I have to say."

Social Web Analytics

We looked at some of the free services that smaller organizations can use to monitor what's being said in real time. Now let's look at more sophisticated platforms that can help larger organizations not only monitor what's being said, but also provide analytics and reports (to share with management) and integrate into your workflow.

Many social-media pros, like Paul Dunay of Avaya and Christopher Barger of GM, rely on both free services and paid analytics applications.

Just a few years ago, Twitter didn't even exist and Facebook was only for those with an *.edu* email address. But the analytics tools are catching up fast and the market is growing quickly.

To understand the quickly evolving landscape, I consulted Philip Sheldrake, founder of Influence Crowd, LPP. Sheldrake shows companies how influence flows and helps them understand what's happening—all in time to react.

First a definition. So far in this chapter, I've used the term "monitoring" to talk about the process of watching what is being said. When you tack on the analytical aspect (creating data, like how many blog posts mentioned a company last week, and doing sentiment analysis, which is a ratio of positive versus negative opinions) you end up with a service that is much more than mere monitoring. It's sort of like the difference between watching a sporting event live versus watching it on TV, complete with statistics and commentary.

This is how Sheldrake describes social Web analytics:

The application of search, indexing, semantic analysis, and business intelligence technologies to the task of identifying, tracking, listening to, and participating in the distributed conversations about a particular brand, product, or issue, with emphasis on quantifying the trend in each conversation's sentiment and influence.

Wow. That's a mouthful! But read it again slowly and it will start to make sense. This is more than just monitoring what people say. Indeed, some organizations are becoming extremely sophisticated in their use of the various available tools.

"Some people use the terms *social Web analytics* and *social media analytics* interchangeably," Sheldrake says. But that's misleading. "Social media is only a subset of the social Web. The social Web encompasses social media (e.g., Facebook, Amazon reviews, blogs), applications (e.g., TweetDeck, Skype), services (e.g., geolocation feeds, like Friendfeed and Taptu), and the network itself. So in the longer term, social Web analytics will increasingly encompass a wider set of data than just social media information; some vendors are already there."

How Social Web Analytics Will Help Your Business

- Gathering and storing data from the social Web, including blogs, forums, and news sites.
- Providing a facility to analyze the data and create meaning. This typically includes delivering information in the form of charts, graphs, and the aforementioned sentiment analyses.
- Presenting the information in easy-to-digest ways to internal constituents, including those charged with responding plus executives who need to be aware of what's being said.
- Integrating the services into companies' normal workflow routines, such as existing customer-management systems or sales-automation systems. (We talk about this at length in Chapter 15.)
- Making it easy to react to the information and follow up over time as appropriate.

A Selection of Social Web Analytics Services

Here is a list of social Web analytics services, both free and commercial. The commercial services run from a few hundred dollars monthly to millions of dollars annually for the most sophisticated global implementations.

Sheldrake says that some pundits maintain lists of more than 200 services that wholly or partially meet our definition of social Web analytics. So please note that this a selection of the more interesting and popular services not a comprehensive list. All these services are available in English, but if you need to handle multilanguage content, study each offering carefully.

As you evaluate each of these, make sure it offers "real time"—the best service speeds are a matter of seconds. Some services (especially those indexing mainstream media sources) only feed news into the system hourly. In a real-time environment, an hour's delay is just not going to work.

Free Services for Mainstream Media and Social Media

- Google, www.google.com
- Bing, www.bing.com
- Yahoo!, www.yahoo.com
- Ask, www.ask.com

Free Graphical Analysis Tools

- BlogPulse, www.blogpulse.com
- Google Trends, www.google.com/trends

Free Services for Blog Search

- Google Blog Search, http://blogsearch.google.com
- Technorati, www.technorati.com
- Twingly, www.twingly.com
- IceRocket, www.icerocket.com

Free Alerting Service

- Google Alerts, www.google.com/alerts

Free Twitter Search

- HootSuite, http://hootsuite.com/
- TweetDeck, www.tweetdeck.com
- Twitter search, http://search.twitter.com

Commercial Services

- Alterian, www.alterian.com/www.techrigy.com
- Attentio, www.attentio.com
- Brandwatch, www.brandwatch.net
- CIC, www.ciccorporate.com
- Cision, www.cision.com
- Crimson Hexagon, www.crimsonhexagon.com
- Collective Intellect, www.collectiveintellect.com
- dna13, www.dna13.com
- Dow Jones, www.dowjones.com/product-djinsight.asp
- Nielsen BuzzMetrics, http://en-us.nielsen.com/tab/product_families/nielsen_buzzmetrics
- Radian6, www.radian6.com
- Scout Labs, www.scoutlabs.com
- Sysomos, www.sysomos.com
- TNS Cymfony, www.cymfony.com
- Trackur, www.trackur.com
- Visible Technologies, www.visibletechnologies.com

Again, this is not a comprehensive list, just a starting point to see what's out there.

The ultimate goal for sophisticated organizations is to seamlessly integrate a social Web analytics platform into the existing work processes of marketing and PR departments so that they become a tool to enable, not just to alert. And everybody has to be on board.

"[Enterprise-wide] process engineering is important here," Sheldrake says. "You have to be vigorous and disciplined. Your top people must say, 'We need to listen, we will converse and we're going to put in place a system that will help us.'"

One key consideration in integrating the system into your organizational structure is to ensure a competent person is assigned to respond appropriately and in real time. It is no trivial task for a large organization to divvy up hundreds of items per day and respond to them. "You don't want a couple of hundred things going to all people on your team, because that's just duplication of effort," Sheldrake says. He says that setting up a system like a telephone support center can work well. New issues are sent to a particular representative for follow-up, and then that issue is "owned" by the rep through completion. Of course, given the realities of the 24-hour, always-on world, fully monitoring in real time around the clock will be a challenge to organizations that will need to do so.

How Even the Biggest Can Be Seamlessly Social

"There are three of us in the corporate social-media team at HQ," Tim Washer, head of social-media productions at IBM told me. "But there are 700 people in communications, and we actively monitor what is being said. So if there is a fast-breaking issue, we make sure that the social-media team member, or public relations or customer service, is aware of the situation. We ask them to respond quickly and to respond in the same media. If it is an issue on a blog, then we want people to respond on the same blog as [the original] comment."

Washer's point on responding via the same media may seem obvious. Sure, you might say, if someone blogs about your company, you should comment on the blog, right? Yes. But many people get tripped up when confronted with media like YouTube videos. What do you do then?

Ideally, you should still respond in that medium. YouTube has a comment feature, but with popular videos there can be hundreds or even thousands of comments, and yours can get lost. Why not quickly film a video response and post it onto your YouTube channel? Depending on the video channel, responses will often appear in the list of related videos that appear when a clip finishes playing, so viewers will have a better chance of finding your response. On YouTube, you can create a link to an existing video marking it as a "response."

You're not limited to responding in one medium. It's often good to respond in multiple media. For example, do a video response plus a blog post with the video embedded.

Monitoring what's being said and using social Web analytics to make reacting to it a part of your organizational culture is critical for any business that is serious about operating in real time. But this requires a huge amount of work, particularly for larger companies.

In Chapter 13, I advocate creating a new position I call "chief real-time communications officer." If you make the challenge a priority on that level, and back it with the best configuration of the tools available for your particular situation, you'll be ready to engage immediately.

When the world talks about you, you will be able to respond with the speed the world now expects—and respects.

9 Tap the Crowd for Quick Action

Each year, the Super Bowl pits the National Football League's top two teams in a championship that is America's most watched event—106.5 million TV viewers in 2010. The audience is so huge that companies go all out to create ads that people remember and talk about. The event is so high profile and the budgets are so enormous that each ad is intensely measured and discussed.

In this way, the Super Bowl is also an advertising championship—and I enjoy the commercial competition more than the football. (Yes, I am a marketing geek.)

I'm always fascinated to see what each company comes up with. Who's investing in Super Bowl ads this year? What products are they talking about? Are they using humor? Celebrity? Drama? Or some other technique?

Each year, I used to watch the game, take notes about the ads, then write a blog post about it first thing the next morning. Many newspapers do the same, sometimes using panels of several "experts" that rank the ads according to various criteria. These articles are often amusing, but they lack something important. They rely on the opinions of just a few people and we don't see them until hours (or even days) after the game is over.

That's why, over the past few years, I began to find the Super Bowl advertising commentary (including my own) somehow weak and unconvincing. Watching the football game itself we know instantly when one team scores a touchdown. The crowd goes wild. At the end of the game, we *know* who won.

So why do we have to wait until the next day to learn who won the advertising competition? In fact, we don't get a clear outcome—just a debate among experts.

With ads as with touchdowns, in real time I want to hear the roar of the crowd—the reaction of 100 million American viewers. That's the real measure of who scored!

With social media that is now fully possible. So I was glad to see Mullen, an ad agency, partner with social-media monitoring and engagement provider Radian6 to create BrandBowl 2010, a real-time competition that gauged reaction to ads on the 2010 Super Bowl. They used Web-based *crowdsourcing* techniques, monitoring and measuring people's opinions, and ranked the ads as the game was being played.

Crowdsourcing involves taking a task usually performed by one or a few people and distributing among a *crowd* of people—outsourcing it to a crowd—via online social networks.

For example, to name a new product you might tap your network of fans and ask them for suggestions. In this way, crowdsourcing might replace weeks of internal head-scratching or hefty fees paid to a specialist naming agency. Alternatively, crowdsourcing might augment the conventional process. Take a shortlist of names vetted for trademark compliance, and ask your fans which ones they like.

How to Title a Book or Name a Product

That's what Mark Levy did to finalize the title of his latest book: *Accidental Genius: Using Writing to Generate Your Best Ideas, Insight, and Content.*

Levy and his publisher used SurveyMonkey, a Web-based survey tool, to solicit input from a crowd of people on the book's title and subtitle. The publisher sent out email questionnaires to Levy's friends, colleagues, and fans asking them to rank their favorites from two lists of titles and subtitles.

"For me, crowdsourcing was interesting in unexpected ways," Levy told me. "As a creative, I was scared that crowdsourcing would force artistic choices on me that I'd hate. In other words, I thought I'd lose control of my own project based on public opinion. Instead, the crowdsourcing backed up something I had suspected (that *Accidental Genius* was the best title), and it gave people a forum to help me construct [a subtitle] I wouldn't have gotten without their input."

This technique is not just for smaller organizations. Kodak used crowd-sourcing to name a new waterproof video camera code named "zx3." The contest quickly crowdsourced thousands of name ideas with the winning name "Kodak PlaySport" selected.

A Crowd for Any Purpose

The best example of an enormous crowdsourced project is Wikipedia, the free online encyclopedia that anybody can add to or edit. Wikipedia has grown rapidly since its creation in 2001 into one of the largest reference web sites, attracting approximately 65 million visitors per month in 2009. Wikipedia has more than 85,000 active contributors working on 14 million articles in more than 260 languages. Every day, people around the world collectively make tens of thousands of real-time edits and create thousands of new articles. Thus, the volume of knowledge held by Wikipedia expands each day, all thanks to one of the most successful crowdsourcing projects on the planet.

Television has also discovered crowdsourcing. During live broadcasts, programs like *American Idol* and *Britain's Got Talent* get audiences to evaluate performers by calling a special phone number or texting their votes. This real-time crowdsourcing attracts and holds the attention of viewers by letting them feel they are actively involved.

> When people help you answer a question via crowdsourcing they feel a sense of ownership. Participation turns spectators into supporters.

Crowdsourcing can also help you make decisions based on massively collective wisdom. With BrandBowl 2010, the opinions of tens of thousands of people, gathered in real time, was a powerful counterpoint to the expert opinion of armchair quarterbacks in the next morning's newspapers. I found the crowdsourced approach so compelling that I didn't even bother to blog my own opinions on the Super Bowl 2010 ads. Instead, I simply tweeted my followers a link to the BrandBowl 2010 site.

BrandBowl used 98,656 tweets collected during the game to determine an overall ranking of the ads. This was based on a composite score that took into consideration both volume (the number of people who tweeted about each ad) and sentiment (as calculated by BrandBowl co-creator Radian6). The opinions expressed in the tweets were used to produce a net sentiment score, calculated as (positive tweets – negative tweets)/total tweets, to measure whether overall public reaction was positive or negative.

To determine whether an individual tweet was positive or negative, Radian6 built a reference library of examples, assigning values to language used in tweets to sort subtle distinctions and colloquial usage (which happens often on Twitter). For example, "That ad was really bad; it truly stunk" would be negative. However, "That ad was bad ass; it was dope" would be positive. After humans created the reference library, an automated system compared online conversation against the benchmark. Thus, on-topic posts were assigned a positive, negative, or neutral designation in real time, based on specified sentiment keywords and phrases.

The BrandBowl 2010 site also included links to the various ads, so anybody who missed one (perhaps fetching more beer) could check it out.

"Crowdsourcing puts forth a problem or a challenge to a whole bunch of people to see if the wisdom of the crowd can come back and nail the thing either more quickly or in a way that you never previously anticipated," says Edward Boches, chief creative officer at Mullen, co-creator of BrandBowl 2010. "For the Super Bowl ads, you didn't have to wait until Monday morning and *USA Today* to know what brands did best, because we had results throughout the game."

The top two brands were Doritos and Google. Doritos won the BrandBowl 2010 title by dominating the sheer volume of tweets. That was enough to keep them ahead of Google, which did have a higher percentage of positive tweets. The most popular brands in the competition were McDonald's and Dr. Pepper. Interestingly, neither of these had the necessary volume to break into the BrandBowl top 10, but the tweets about these brands were overwhelmingly positive. The last-place finisher in BrandBowl 2010 was Budweiser Select55.

Many reporters who covered the Super Bowl advertisements in print and online cited the results of BrandBowl 2010 in their stories, including writers for the *San Francisco Chronicle*, the *Boston Globe*, and *AdWeek*. I find it fascinating but hardly surprising that the real-time crowdsourced results were so widely cited in the conventional coverage. Clearly, people are starting to recognize the value of real-time crowdsourcing.

Finding the Right Crowd

Many organizations are discovering that crowdsourcing produces outcomes *much* faster than traditional methods. Here are some tasks or projects that you might consider crowdsourcing.

- Generate a wide variety of solutions or answers to a question.
- Solicit suggestions from your supporters, for example, new product names.
- Encourage people to vote on or rank a list of items (e.g., select a contest winner).
- Slice large, labor-intensive projects into many small tasks that volunteers can easily accomplish.
- Generate submissions to a contest.
- Tap a large number of expert opinions quickly.
- Solicit donations of time or money to a worthy cause.
- Generate interest in attending a physical meeting or event.

As a first step into crowdsourcing, consider asking your network a question. If you have an existing presence in a social network (e.g., LinkedIn, Facebook, or Twitter), you can do this right now.

> Crowdsourcing has potential to generate instant and meaningful results you can use right away.

At our family Christmas Eve in 2009, my brother Peter told us he was skeptical about Twitter. He had read about it but just couldn't figure out why anyone would want to tweet. Rather than offer my own explanation, I decided to send out a tweet asking others for answers. The response exceeded my expectations.

My tweet read: *My brother Peter doesn't understand Twitter. "It's weird - who cares what you do?" Can you guys help explain please!!*

I started receiving replies in seconds. Within 10 minutes, I had 50 responses from people all over the world, including Coogee, Australia, and

Santo Domingo in the Dominican Republic. And all of this was happening in real time on Christmas Eve!

I just love the answers that came back. I'm still laughing at some, and others are rather profound.

- *Twitter is like personal hygiene. You only find out about the benefits after you start . . .*
- *It's a search engine for life. You want to find people who like to do what you do? Search, listen and connect.*
- *Twitter is like mingling at a party with some people you know, others you don't, and many more you have yet to meet.*
- *Nope, he's right. It's weird. We're weird. Life is weird. There we go, full circle.;)*
- *Replying just to show Peter that people are listening.*
- *Twitter, for me, is more about quickly sharing ideas and picking brains of other people.*
- *Twitter is the replacement for the people that you'd like to talk to and learn from when you can't be there with them.*
- *It's not so much about what you do but more around what you think.*
- *It's a great way to share ideas and connect with all kinds of interesting people. And, it can be fun.*
- *Twitter gets you access to ideas from 100s of people - in any topic that interests you.*
- *Share and discover interesting stuff, find interesting people and follow their interests.*
- *Twitter is the largest focus group in the world, and also free! You can know exactly the thoughts of your prospects in real time!*

Isn't it amazing, the different ways 50 people can answer something, each in 140 characters or fewer and in just a few minutes. You end up with a better explanation than any one person could possibly think up in days of contemplation! That's the power of crowdsourcing. If you've got a nagging question you need answered in real time, why not put it out to your supporters and see what they have to say *right now*?

In the interest of full disclosure: Peter is still skeptical. But he understands much more about Twitter than he did before, because of the many real-time responses I got to my query. Thanks, everybody!

Massive Brainstorm

One use of crowdsourcing that is increasingly popular (especially for consumer brands) is to run contests that give creative people a chance to submit promotional ideas—videos, images, logos, you name it. You often get stunning creativity. Even better, it's often ready to use off the shelf without the lengthy process required with an in-house team or an outside agency.

Young, talented creative people are so eager to get ahead that many welcome the chance to produce work for a major brand. Contests offer them a chance for exposure. Or maybe you'll be so impressed that you hire them. At very least, contestants come out with a piece to add to their portfolio.

HP, the Silicon Valley IT giant, took this approach, asking students to: "Present an idea that promotes HP Workstations' ability to bring to life anything the creative mind can conceive."

One of the responses to this challenge—filmed, edited, and directed by Matt Robinson and Tom Wrigglesworth—is among my all-time favorite online videos. In it, the creators used time-lapse videography to capture HP printers spitting out documents in time with a dance beat. The video is just terrific! Have a look.

Heineken, Holland's famous brewer, solicited video submissions for a sequel to the company's "walking refrigerator" TV commercial that was seen around the world. Heineken asked BrandFighters, a crowdsourcing specialist, to organize the contest and spread the word via social media. Contestants of legal drinking age were given six weeks to plan, produce, shoot, and edit a one-minute video. Heineken picked the winner from 35 entries received.

Jan-Paul de Beer, who came up with the concept for BrandFighters, says filmmakers are eager to enter contests in order to get exposure. "How else can a young filmmaker have an opportunity to make a film for a big brand?" he told me.

Perhaps the best feature of efforts like this is the opportunity it gives a brand to interact with its target demographics. You get brilliant members of your target audience to impress their peers.

Crowdsourcing a Movie for Free

Also in the Netherlands, I found another example that takes crowdsourcing to the extreme. Jan Willem Alphenaar, producer and director of *DSB the*

Movie, managed to produce a two-hour documentary in record time—and with zero budget!

The film tells the story of DSB Bank NV, a Dutch bank that went bankrupt in October 2009. Amazingly, Alphenaar crowdsourced everything needed for the film—logo, script, soundtrack, editing, camera work, acting, and publicity—for free! And where comparable productions take a year to produce, *DSB the Movie* was completed in just four months.

Alphenaar put the word out through LinkedIn, Twitter, and Hyves, a Dutch-language social networking site. "I first called to the crowd to get a logo," Alphenaar says. "It was also a test to see if our system would work and if the audience understood what we expected from them. We ended up with 42 logo designs in five days."

Imagine that. Alphenaar was able to choose the first crowdsourced component from among 42 designs submitted in a mere five days. When I worked on a logo project at a previous employer it took us months to get that far!

Next task was to crowdsource a script. "We had two professional script writers who said, 'Hey, we will help. This is a nice project. We can make a name with that,'" Alphenaar recounts.

But in order to create a script, the writers needed input from former DSB clients and staff, and people involved in the bankruptcy process. So Alphenaar put out another call, this time for script input. "We talked with ex-employees of the bank and with people from the government, and everybody gave us information," he says.

Soon a journalist from *Quote*, a Dutch business publication, saw the *DSB the Movie* group on LinkedIn while doing research on the DSB Bank failure. He contacted Alphenaar to say he was intrigued by the movie and wrote a story that was published online. When that tipped off other journalists covering the scandal, online stories began to snowball.

"The next day we were on the front page of *De Telegraaf*, the largest newspaper in the Netherlands, as well as on *BNR Nieuwsradio, Marketing Tribune, Mediajournaal, EindhovensDagblad*, and more. We were all over the news," Alphenaar says.

This heightened profile served to expand the pool of crowdsource contributors.

Naturally, when it came time to start filming that, too, was crowdsourced. People interested in doing a scene were given the script, asked to film it, then upload the results to YouTube. "Every scene had five to eight contributions, and the audience [the crowd following the film's progress] voted online to decide which one to use," Alphenaar says.

When the soundtrack was crowdsourced, voters likewise evaluated three submissions from professional musicians.

Alphenaar's project shows how even a large undertaking can be crowdsourced and completed in a fraction of the time conventional efforts require. Although the overall effort still took time, each element was created extremely quickly.

For example, when I first spoke with Alphenaar, there was no English-language site for the film. Once I pointed this out, he said he'd get one produced. Imagine my surprise when he contacted me a few hours later to say translation had already been crowdsourced and that an English-language version would go live next day. Wow, talk about real-time speed!

"Your audience is willing to help you," Alphenaar says. "They don't need money, they just want credit. Normally you need a year and lots of money to make a movie. We don't have money at all. And we don't want to earn money on this movie, because it's from the crowds, for the crowds. I think crowdsourcing has a big future in marketing, because your audience is willing to help you with your products, with your ideas. And they are willing to help you if they get the credit. They just want to help and be complimented for what they did."

You Gotta Give to Get

All of this crowdsourcing stuff sounds great, doesn't it? Who wouldn't be thrilled to put out a call to the crowd and have contributors send you valuable material quickly and for free?

Take note, though, that none of this just happens. As you may have noticed throughout this chapter, it's important to consider what benefit contributors will receive for their efforts.

With *DSB the Movie*, contributors got to feel integrally involved in making an important film, one that chronicled a story that affected many people in the Netherlands. In a sense, they traded work for bragging rights and a credit in the film.

The young filmmakers who submitted short videos for Heineken had an opportunity to have their work showcased to marketing managers at one of the most famous brands in the world, getting their foot in a door that is normally closed.

So before you ask for help, make sure you can offer contributors some tangible reward for their efforts.

Sometimes, all it takes is a simple "thank you" when people take time to help you. When I asked my Twitter followers to help explain Twitter to my brother Peter, the 50 or so people who answered got my thanks by way of mention in the blog post where I talked about the Q&A exchange.

My point in telling you about crowdsourcing is not to show how you can procure goods and services on the cheap—although that may be a secondary benefit. Maybe this can work best in a society with a high level of shared trust—in countries like the Netherlands or Japan. In the United States all it will take to cripple crowdsourcing is for it to develop a bad reputation by a few sharp sleazebags who rip off their contributors, email spam-like, trying to get something for nothing.

Here's hoping that crowdsourcing grows on the strength of respect and trust.

What I find fascinating and relevant about crowdsourcing is how it can allow you to gain knowledge and insight, and to create quality content, *much more quickly* than with a conventional approach. That's what this book is all about: connecting with your customers and speeding up the pace of your business.

Connect with Your Market

Is there anything more impersonal or unfriendly than, "Please choose from the following eight options," followed by 10 minutes of hold music? Sadly, an automated telephone attendant, plus maybe an email form on the web site, is all that connects most companies to their customers. C'mon, people, can't we do better than that?

In fact, today any company *can* do better that—and grow the business by doing it. As smart companies are learning, social media and mobile devices are creating huge opportunities for real-time response and proactive contact with customers.

In Part Two we look at a variety of real-time ways to communicate with your customers. We also explore how speed leads to growth when innovative services save customers' time and shorter development lead times get new products to market first.

10 Real-Time Customer Connection

My friend Justin Locke tells a great story about connecting with customers. Locke is author of *Real Men Don't Rehearse*, a hysterical memoir of his years as a bassist with the Boston Pops Orchestra. I'll let Justin tell it in his own words:

In the first two or three summers of concerts, the politics, seniority, and fate in general added up to my being the third chair bass player. Since the first two bass players were in front of the rest of the section, that meant that I was placed behind them, right on the very edge of the stage. If I looked down to my left, I would see one or two tables of people in the audience who, even though they were "in the front row," didn't have much of a view of anything other than my Allen Edmonds shoelaces. I always thought of people in the audience as guests in my home, so once I picked up my bass and started to warm up, I would always look down, catch their eye, and say, "Hello, my name is Justin, and I will be your bass player this evening." This always, always, always got a laugh from these people who were feeling a bit out of place in an unfamiliar environment . . . and not in the best seating arrangement. Many's the night they offered to buy me drinks.

Once management caught wind of the fact that I, unlike everyone else in the orchestra, was making eye contact and actually conversing with "those people" out in the audience, I was immediately demoted to fifth chair, where I could no longer cause such discrepancies in the space-time continuum.

I love this story because it perfectly illustrates management's reflexive impulse to create barriers between employees and customers, thereby eliminating any chance that humanity might somehow creep into the dialogue and shatter the illusion of robotic uniformity.

Beyond avoiding any trace of humanity, too many companies go to great lengths to hide from their customers. They put you through phone tree hell if you try to call. And if you use the anonymous "contact us" forms on their fancy web sites your email goes into a black hole.

Does *anyone* like doing business with a company like this? I don't know about you, but I spend every minute on hold thinking about which competitor I'd like to switch to.

Connecting with Customers *Is* Marketing and PR

So far in this book we've focused on using real-time marketing and PR to engage the world at large: potential customers, the media, the blogosphere, and others. Here's where we get to a constituency that matters even more: your *existing customers*—the people you count on to come for more; the people who tell others what it's really like to deal with you.

Understanding that current customers need to know they are appreciated, smart companies are working to demonstrate that by responding with both speed and personal care. In this chapter we look at a number of ways to go about this.

Great customer service is the essential platform on which every other marketing and PR activity is built. After all, if your existing customers don't have good things to tell friends, family, and social-media contacts about their experiences, no amount of advertising can paper over the hole in your offering. But when your customers' experiences are surprisingly exceptional, when they exceed their expectations, they want to tell the world.

If the experience is: "I paid an average price; it works okay, I guess; and customer service was about what I expected"—who's going to bother sharing that? But if you surprise and delight customers—with unbeatable value, outstanding performance, random acts of kindness, quick response, or just being human—they naturally want to share the experience. The point is that social media now give customers a powerful outlet with which to share their experiences, whether it's venting frustration or lavishing praise. Now more than ever, nothing builds business better than a terrific referral from a happy customer.

There are four key contact points where companies need to focus on creating or improving real-time connections with customers.

1. **Presale:** Many companies focus all their efforts on presale connection with potential customers, too often neglecting the rest of the sales cycle. And because the first section of the book was focused on presale, enough said here.
2. **Immediate postsale:** What you say to a new customer immediately after the sale sets the tone for the rest of the relationship. So speak up right away to build trust.
3. **Ready to receive:** Whether after-sale customer inquiries are rare or daily occurrences in your business, both sides win when the outcome is customer-satisfaction delivered swiftly. The company wins even more when the lessons are learned from each contact. If your baggage-handlers are tossing guitars, fix the problem and the guitar!
4. **Problem resolution and crisis communication:** If a serious problem arises, chances are that your first alert will come from a customer. So if a user calls saying her accelerator is sticking, don't just respond, "It must be the floor mat, ma'am." Listen closely and check it out quickly. If it turns out to be a widespread problem, waste no time in telling customers. It is essential that they hear about it from you first, quickly and accurately.

Let's look at how various companies are developing real-time response mechanisms for each of these after-sales contact points. You may find that some are relevant to your business. But then again, there is no hard and fast "right way" to connect. Keep the goal in mind and develop your own approach. Succeed at this and you may find yourself out in front of your industry, simply because so few companies have even begun to ask the right questions.

Why Should *I* Help *You*?

Each year I travel all over the world, speaking to business audiences about the types of ideas you're reading here. That means I stay in a heck of a lot of hotels—40 or more a year. And because I do my own reservations online, I'm in an excellent position to observe how hotels communicate with customers after reservation are made.

Nearly all hotels send confirmation by email soon after the booking is made. And a few send reminders a week or so before check-in. Typically, that's all I get *before* a stay.

Many hotels, though, bug me *after* a stay to request that I fill out a survey about my experience. I received this email, ostensibly from Rakesh Sarna, a Hyatt executive, as I wrote this chapter:

> I would like to take this opportunity to thank you for your stay with us at Grand Hyatt Mumbai from February 07 to February 11. We were delighted to have you as our guest and hope that your stay was most enjoyable.
>
> Recently we invited you to complete a short survey regarding your stay. As a valued Gold Passport Member, we would be most grateful if you would take the time to provide us with your valuable feedback. This will be most helpful in assisting us to continue to refine and improve our level of service.

I never do these surveys because they are time-consuming for me and a lazy way for the hotels to get feedback. Note that Rakesh is talking about what *he* wants from *me*! How egotistical is that? Surveys might benefit companies, but they frequently piss off customers.

In all your communication, think how it benefits the customer, not what's in it for you.

Thus, it was with interest that I spoke to Wayne Townsend, CEO of ClickSquared, a provider of real-time relationship applications, including sophisticated email systems. As a self-proclaimed expert in booking hotel stays, I asked Townsend to explain how the hotels his company works with connect with customers in real time.

ClickSquared's hotel and resort clients include Montage Laguna Beach Resort and Montage Beverly Hills, both high-end Southern California luxury resorts featuring spas and extra amenities. Customers typically reserve three or four months in advance, and stay three nights in a deluxe room. "We're integrated with the hotel's property management and reservation systems," Townsend says. "We send an email confirmation saying, 'We got your reservation, here's your itinerary, and here's a special deal: Would you like an extra night? Would you like a bigger room? Would you like to book a spa treatment?' The confirmation emails are sent in real time as a reservation is made."

After the initial confirmation, customers receive a series of messages as the stay approaches. "What we have found with our clients is that if we can get the right information out at the right time using the communication channel customers prefer, we can get three- to five-times better response rates," Townsend says. In other words, this focus on timely delivery generates much better "open rates" for email, as well as better responses to offers than the typical generic email most organizations send.

Townsend says that optimizing the timing of a hotel prestay program requires adjustments based on how far in advance each person is booking. The program gets compressed, with certain email dropping out, when the booking takes place shortly before the stay. It gets extended, with email being added, if the booking takes place early.

"There's a lot of focus on ensuring the communications remain relevant," he says. "If the guest adds a spa reservation or a tee-time at a golf course, we adjust their itinerary right away, we confirm it again, and we communicate something relevant such as weather information." This real-time approach requires sophisticated communication automation tightly integrated with the hotel's reservations systems. For example, if somebody makes a golf reservation by phone rather than online, this information is also added to the customer record and triggers an instant adjustment to the email communications program. I like this because I hate it when a hotel sends out an offer for something like golf when you're already booked for golf. When this happens, I roll my eyes and say "duh!" or something more colorful. Because this contextual information specific to each person's visit is updated constantly, communication is timely, relevant, and appreciated.

Clearly, connecting with customers in real time after a sale is an essential component to good marketing. After all, when someone has a great experience right after booking, they're engaged even before the actual stay. That's all the more valuable considering that people can usually cancel their reservations and go elsewhere. Effective communications help keep the guest "warm" between booking and check-in.

Interacting with Customers in Real Time

Finding ways to interact with customers on a regular basis and in real time is something of an art form. But if you have the right creative approach social media can now make communication instant, easy, and free.

Chris Reimer is the founder and proprietor of Rizzo Tees, an e-commerce site that sells hip original-design T-shirts. Reimer constantly connects with his customers through social networks. "I love interacting with people," Reimer says. "That makes this a very fun business to be in. Email me, find me on Twitter and Facebook, talk to me, tell me what's on your mind. The more people I get to 'meet,' the better. It's easy to talk about a subject I like, like T-shirts, and it's easy to get people interested because it's a fun topic."

For Reimer, Twitter is a key after-sales communication tool. "There's nothing cooler than when someone tweets a photo of themselves wearing one of my shirts," he says. "I have no shame about immediately retweeting things like that, then following up with thanks to that person."

I know this to be true because when I tweeted *Friends don't let friends tweet and drive via @RizzoTees (on a t-shirt) http://www.rizzotees.com/,* Reimer tweeted back just seconds later *@dmscott hahaaaa thanks man! you are too kind.*

I'm also fascinated by the way Reimer uses crowdsourcing. "A lot of the designs are of my own imagination," he says. "With a new design, I'll post it to my blog and say, 'What do you guys think about this?' And then I'll tweet it to my nearly 40,000 followers. For example, my graphic designer nailed a great design for a Kate Gosselin shirt, a silhouette that shows her hairstyle. But I had this tagline: $(Jon + Kate + 8) - (Jon \times GF)/2 = \_\_\_$. So I asked people and, man, it got panned! No one liked it! They said, 'This is confusing—I mean I get the picture, but what's with the algebraic formula?' So I asked for suggestions. And when someone tweeted back '*Mullet 2.0*,' others said right away, 'Hey, that's actually pretty good!' So we went with it."

Reimer says he can get feedback on T-shirt designs in just a few minutes. "People jump in to save me from printing something that wouldn't sell and would make my company look bad," he says. "I'll tell them, 'Be honest with me.' You don't want a bunch of yes-men telling you, 'Hey it's great.' Getting instant feedback saves me from wasting thousands of dollars and losing face."

Reimer is a solo-entrepreneur, running his business from his basement and using freelance designers. "I have no partner," he says. "Except for my wife who sometimes comes up with tee ideas, it's just me. People say, 'You need a partner,' and I say, 'No I don't.' I have nearly 40,000 followers on Twitter, and they are my partners, because I rely on them for honest advice in the same way I might rely on a true partner."

Friends Tweet Friends First

You know what I absolutely hate? It just burns me up when a company I buy from offers new customers a better deal to sign up than I get as someone who has been their customer for years. Magazines and newspapers do this all the time. I'll renew my $50-per-month subscription to the *Boston Globe* newspaper only to see *Special Introductory Offer: Sign up for home delivery of* the Boston Globe *and save 50% off the home delivery rate.* Well, shoot! What about me? And don't get me started on the mobile phone companies and their amazing pricing that everyone *except* existing customers qualifies for!

I think companies should do the exact opposite. Tell your fans first. Give your best deals to existing customers. Don't let people who pay you today see you don't care!

In my opinion, the most famous tweet of all time occurred early on the morning of Saturday, August 23, 2008. I was on vacation, and like I do first thing most mornings, I checked Twitter when I woke up. I could see immediately that people were buzzing about Barack Obama's choice of vice-presidential running mate. So I high-tailed it over to @BarackObama, and saw this tweet: *Announcing Senator Joe Biden as our VP nominee. Watch the first Obama-Biden rally live at 3pm ET on http://BarackObama.com.*

Although Obama's choosing Biden was interesting, the marketing geek in me was absolutely fascinated to learn that the tweet was sent 10 minutes *before* the press release alerting the media. Holy cow! The Obama campaign alerted their most important supporters *first*!

This is an essential lesson in the art of real-time customer connection. In his book *The Audacity to Win*, David Plouffe, Obama's campaign manager, writes of the decision to inform supporters of the Biden pick first and via Twitter: "[I]t was consistent with other key junctures in the campaign—reporting fund-raising numbers, the decision to limit our primary debates, opting out of the public funding system—where we had communicated first directly to our supporters. This was their campaign as much as ours, and they deserved to get a heads-up from us about important decisions."

It was this kind of attention to his base that got Barack Obama elected. The lesson here is to stop focusing on providing better service and pricing to non-customers (as mobile phone providers and magazines do) and instead favor those who favor you: your existing customers.

Embracing the Tweet

In researching this book, I came across many examples where Twitter is used as a real-time channel to alert customers to fast-changing information and special deals. Of course, there are many other ways to reach people, but Twitter is growing in popularity among marketers and audiences alike. Marketers like it because it is so easy to do; audiences like it because they can choose what and when they want to follow.

Your challenge in replicating these ideas is to deliver information that *your buyers* value as important. If you try to use Twitter to hype your offering in a way that seems sleazy or overly self-serving, you risk doing your company harm.

So study these ideas, think about your customers' needs, and come up with valuable information you can serve up in real time.

The Cookies Are Ready!

Albion Cafe in Shoreditch, London, sends a tweet (Twitter ID: @albionsoven) when baked goods come fresh and hot from the oven. Example: *Freshly baked crumbly Chocolate Chip Cookies stuffed with oozy chocolate chips. http://bakertweet.com/m/721* (the URL points to a photo of the cookies). Locals subscribe so they know exactly when to pop over. Albion Cafe uses

BakerTweet, a tool that makes it easy for bakers to tweet when something is fresh out of the oven.

Red Tag Promotion

As 2009 neared its end, marketers at telecom-equipment supplier Avaya Inc. helped their colleagues in sales end the year on a bright note. The "Red Tag Promotion" offered customers who placed an order and completed the purchase by year-end a 40 percent discount on the expertise of Avaya's technology architects. It was a good deal, but only available within a small time window. The tweet, *Expert Avaya Communications Resources – 'Red Tag' Promo for Partners/Customers – up to 40% discounts – DM if interested,* gave the sales reps a welcome boost in the critical year-end period. (Note that, unlike the *Boston Globe* example mentioned earlier, this offer was open to existing customers too!)

Soon to Be Expired

Kenko.com, Japan's number-one online drug store, offers a range of products that dwarfs the selection at its bricks-and-mortar competitors. But with so many products on offer, CEO Genri Goto told me he has to make sure that his people stay on top of inventory management. If they allow products to expire, the entire lot must be destroyed unsold. Happily, Kenko.com harnessed Twitter to solve inventory problems and delight customers in one go.

As soon as the Kenko.com warehouse manager decides that a product lot is unlikely to sell before its expiry date, he immediately notifies his online sales counterpart. Wasting no time, the sales manager immediately tweets customers a special clearance offer via a dedicated Twitter ID @kenkocom_soko as well as via email and SMS.

Yes! Tickets Are Available

New York City's nonprofit Theatre Development Fund operates a network of TKTS discount booths, offering same-day tickets to Broadway and Off-Broadway musicals and plays at up to 50 percent off. Customers can subscribe to the TKTS Twitter feed @TDFNYC and receive alerts each day on what shows are available that evening. As I write, today's tweet touts: *A Behanding* in *Spokane, Chicago, Fela!, Hair, Memphis, Next Fall, Race, Rock of Ages, South Pacific, Miracle Worker.* These tweets allow theater customers to know what's available in real time, so they can plan their evening before visiting the ticket booth.

The Ferry Is Delayed

Passengers traveling on Red Funnel Ferries between Southampton and Cowes on the Isle of Wight can receive updates as vessels enter and leave port. The system relies on the ferry's real-time GPS coordinates (public domain information), uploaded into technology designed by Dr. Andy Stanford-Clark, an Isle of Wight resident and IBM master inventor. Stanford-Clark created the automated system because he was frustrated by delays with the Red Funnel ferries he rides to work every day. Tweets from @red_ferries such as *07:30 – Red Eagle is leaving Southampton* proved so popular with passengers that the system has been taken over by the ferry company, with the real-time updates made available on a Web page and via SMS as well as the Twitter feed.

Having Fun in the Snow

Delta Vacations, the airline's package-tour business unit, frequently tweets special vacation deals at Twitter ID @DeltaVacations. When Delta's Minneapolis/St. Paul hub was threatened by a major snowstorm, people started talking about it on Twitter using the hashtag #Snowmaggedon (see Chapter 6 for more on hashtags).

Reacting in real time, Delta Vacations created a promotion that morning for $10 off a customer's next vacation for every inch of snow that fell on the Twin Cities. The #Snowmaggedon hashtag caught on and became a trending topic (one of the most talked about subjects) on Twitter, and the Delta Vacation tweets were the most retweeted in the #Snowmaggedon topic that day. When the snowfall ended with six inches on the ground, Delta Vacations tweeted a promotional code for a $60 discount.

Create Something Retweet Worthy

An important aspect of Twitter is that when you say something interesting, many people will retweet it to their network in real-time, extending your reach into the thousands or even millions of people. If you're clever, you can craft something that is retweet worthy, creating a real-time twitterstorm.

For example, marketers at Cisco create funny videos that promote the Cisco ASR 9000 Series Aggregation Services Routers as a perfect gift for Valentines Day and Fathers' Day. The ridiculous nature of the holiday gift idea videos—giving your father a technology designed for telecommunications companies that will cost a minimum of around $80,000 (instead of a necktie) is hysterical. The videos get tweeted and retweeted generating tens of thousands of views in the days leading up to the holiday.

Let Followers Feel the Love on Twitter

Several times while writing this book, I stayed at the Roger Smith Hotel in New York City. This hostelry has become known by many as being "Twitter friendly," offering special benefits for people who connect with the hotel via Twitter and other social media like Foursquare. Marketers at the hotel monitor Twitter in real time and connect with people who mention the Roger Smith. (Note to those planning a NYC visit: Book your room through the link on the @rshotel Twitter page and get an additional 10 percent off the lowest published room prices.)

But there's more. The hotel links its online customer support with offline interaction. For example, when someone books through Twitter, there is a handwritten card waiting in the room upon check-in, signed with the @rshotel Twitter ID. The hotel frequently hosts "Tweetups" (events where people who know each other in the virtual world of Twitter meet up in real life). These personal touches make it likely that, when people like me check into the hotel, we tweet about the experience, thus building the Roger Smith Hotel's Twitter-friendly reputation even more. For example, the last time I visited, I tweeted a photo of my room: *My awesome room at @rshotel in NYC. Go to their page for Twitter discount. http://yfrog.com/2ea4qj*

These efforts are paying off, according to the hotel's new-media marketing manager, Adam Wallace. "We have started to see substantial returns from our social-media efforts, particularly from Twitter," Wallace says. "Social media is now one of our top revenue generators for rooms, beating out many of the online travel agencies and other channels. The relationships that we have built online have led to a large increase in events business, nearly doubling events revenue. Our restaurant and bar are now regularly buzzing with a crowd of social-media contacts. With each of these areas, there is a certain amount of business that is trackable. And we believe that there is also a lot of business coming in through the overall exposure that we are not able to track. With the amazing loyalty that we have seen from the people that we are connected with online, we expect the revenue numbers in all areas to continue to increase."

How Can You Fight a Fire after the House Burns Down?

April 13, 2009: YouTube user uploads video of a Domino's Pizza employee preparing meals while putting cheese up his nose.

November 9, 2009: The U.S. Consumer Product Safety Commission says consumers should stop using Maclaren baby strollers because hinge mechanisms tend to amputate children's fingertips when users unfold and open the stroller.

January 21, 2010: Toyota files voluntary safety recall on select vehicles for sticking accelerator pedal.

February 24, 2010: Killer whale at SeaWorld in Orlando attacks and kills a trainer after a show.

> No one is immune—so expect and plan for crisis in your shop. You need to react in real time, speaking openly and honestly.

There's no telling what bizarre development may suddenly threaten your company's reputation. What crisis-planning exercise could have anticipated some idiot would let himself be videoed with cheese stuffed up his nose? Who would have thought that Toyota, legendary for quality, would be reduced to "just another car company" in just six months?

No one is immune. And no one can anticipate every disaster scenario. But every company needs to be prepared. So what should you do?

Although a complete crisis communication plan is beyond the scope of this book, I do want to point out how in some key aspects the real-time environment has altered the challenge of crisis planning.

First and foremost, you should fully expect the crisis itself or public reaction to it will flare up first and most dramatically on social media—like the dude with cheese up his nose on YouTube. You should anticipate that it will occur outside business hours and amplify very, very quickly. And you should be prepared to respond flexibly and with lightning speed. Here are nine contingency measures to consider:

1. Assign a crisis-communication team and a lead crisis-communication officer for your organization. The team should include senior executives with full power to make decisions on the spot, the heads of PR and HR, plus the chief real-time communications officer (see Chapter 13 for more on this role in a company). Also assign back-ups to be available when key team members are unavailable.
2. Now, before you need it, gather the contact information for key people in your organization. Get home phone numbers, mobile numbers, vacation home numbers, private email addresses, Twitter IDs, and any other relevant means of quickly reaching people day or night, weekday or weekend.
3. As soon as a crisis situation is apparent, quickly gather facts and plan an initial comment. Make some kind of statement very quickly, even if only: "We are investigating the situation now and will provide an update as soon as we can, but no later than 3 P.M. today."
4. Assign a primary spokesperson who will be the lead communicator.
5. Do not ignore a situation. Never lie. Always be honest and forthright.
6. *Get information out as quickly as possible!*
7. Provide continuous updates throughout the course of the situation.
8. Remember, lawyers are not communicators. The opinion of your legal staff should be considered, but final decisions should be made by competent real-time communicators. Don't let lawyers dictate your communication strategy!
9. Communicate via multiple channels—web site, blog, Twitter feed, media advisories, telephone conference calls, and so on.

Again, this is not intended to be a comprehensive list, but issues to consider in formulating a real-time crisis communications plan. If you have not already done so, do this *now*. You may need to implement the plan sooner than you think.

Meet Your Critics on Their Turf

The corporate crisis-communication playbook urgently needs updating to reflect the new realities of social media. Playbooks written by PR professionals whose expertise predates social media are now, in a word, obsolete. It is no longer enough to rely on the standard tools of mainstream-media relations: live news conferences, press releases, and media advisories.

Social media today are, if not the spawning grounds for crises, the places where the fire spreads first and fastest. But it's also the place where the fire retardant lies. That's where you need to engage—quickly and skillfully—using both media you control (your web site) and open forums.

Here's one of the most common mistakes I see: An organization faces a crisis stemming from information that first appeared on social media, but the company officials choose to respond via mainstream media instead, usually by issuing a press release. Don't make that mistake! If a crisis breaks on a blog, go to that blog and leave a comment right away. If a crisis breaks because of a YouTube video, have your CEO film a one-minute YouTube video in response and post it immediately. If people in your industry forum are talking about defects in your product, jump onto that forum now to respond. You can always grant interviews to mainstream media reporters in addition to this more important follow-up, but don't underestimate the need to jump in at the places where people are already talking.

A major reason for communicating in the forum where the issue first breaks is that the same people who are talking up the initial crisis will then spread the word that you've commented on the situation. In addition, people who get word of the situation and flock to the source to take a look will also see your comment.

Put the CEO to Work

When a crisis unfolds, it is often best to get your chief executive out in front of the situation as primary spokesperson.

Paul F. Levy is president and CEO of Boston's Beth Israel Deaconess Medical Center, an academic medical center affiliated with Harvard Medical School. Levy uses his blog, *Running a Hospital*, as well as Twitter and Facebook, to communicate to his 7,000 employees, half a million patients, the media, the Boston community, and health-care professionals around the world.

Levy, who is highly attuned to real-time communication, sometimes tackles tough subjects such as infection and hygiene rates at the hospitals he oversees. This kind of transparency is unusual in hospital communication, especially coming directly from the CEO on a blog.

In July 2008, Levy faced a crisis when an experienced surgeon operated on the wrong side of a patient during elective surgery. Details of the case were not released (due to patient confidentiality), but Levy knew he had to acknowledge the issue immediately to employees and to the public.

"This was a very big mistake," Levy told me about the wrong side surgery. "Right away we did a fairly quick, but intense, internal analysis of what went wrong. At that meeting, I suggested there were enough lessons from this particular case that we should send it out to the whole hospital, because we knew we needed to fix a systemic problem. I remember saying to the chiefs at that point that if we do send an email to 7,000 people, it would be worldwide in about five seconds, so we should be comfortable with that decision. And to their credit, the chiefs said, 'Absolutely, that is what we should do.'"

So in order to get the information out quickly and as widely as possible, Levy sent the email out simultaneously to hospital employees and local Boston media. He also put out a blog post.

Levy was smart enough to know the news could not be kept under wraps so he made sure the story came from the hospital itself. And as a blogging CEO, Levy already had a large following among patients, employees, and the Boston media. So when it came time to communicate quickly during an unfolding crisis, he had already built trust.

"When we put out the story, one could think it was just some manipulation to inoculate the hospital against bad publicity," he says. "But the fact was that I had published infection rates and hand hygiene rates and stuff like that before on my blog. That gave it more credibility and a sense of honesty."

It Can Happen to *You*!

Reading all these horror stories about the bad stuff that happens to big organizations, if you're a solo entrepreneur (like me) you may be tempted to think you're immune to all this. If so, I have news for you—you're not immune. I certainly wasn't.

As I was writing this chapter, I sent a tweet in response to an email pitch I received from Mktgbuzz. It offered 50 percent off a PRWeb press release for the first 500 people who filled out a form, and I thought the offer might interest my readers.

Very soon after I sent the tweet, @PRWeb tweeted that the organization making the offer was not a PRWeb-sanctioned partner. Although PRWeb does have several affiliate programs Mktgbuzz was not a participant in any of them.

Uh oh!

I wish I had scrutinized the offer more carefully before tweeting. And now I realize I've just sent 40,000 Twitter followers a link to an unauthorized offer. I'm imagining people sending money somewhere they shouldn't because I steered them wrong. I screwed up. And I need to fix it. *Now*.

You can't take back a tweet. Yes, you can delete it, but once a tweet makes it into the various Twitter clients, search engines, gets retweeted, and so on, it never completely disappears. Plus, simply deleting the offending tweet and hoping the problem goes away is contrary to the spirit of transparency I believe we need to maintain on the social Web. So I knew I had to communicate. And quickly! But how?

As soon as I saw the PRWeb tweet, I contacted the person at Mktgbuzz who had sent me the pitch, asking for clarification.

Then I tweeted several times to report what I was hearing from PRWeb. I also sent direct messages to people who contacted me about the offer.

Mktgbuzz quickly removed the offer and also tweeted that they were refunding customers' money. Phew!

I then quickly wrote a blog post under the heading *You cannot take back a tweet*. At the same time, PRWeb posted information on their blog, and we linked to each other's posts.

The entire thing went down in just a few hours. And despite some nervous moments, everything worked out in the end. Customers' money was refunded, and my reputation was not much worse for the wear.

I was thrilled that several people, including Frank from PRWeb and Tess from mktgBUZZ, took the time to comment on my blog in real time. This discussion turned the incident into a good case study in how a situation like this unfolds.

Here are some of the comments left on my blog:

- *A good example of a brand taking years to build but can be hurt in a single instant. Luckily, you published this blog post and the "right" people know you're still a trusted source of information!*
- *This is what I would call "having to take control of the story" that is your business. If PRWeb didn't keep an eye out, they could have had to respond to a "giant snowball" of ticked-off clients. Wow . . . the online world does move FAST.*
- *You may not be able to take back a tweet—but you can be honest about the error and the remedy. You handled this beautifully.*
- *It sounds as if you've tried to right the wrong. I hope your followers understand.*

I'm absolutely convinced that if I hadn't been paying attention to Twitter at the time, or if I had seen the situation unfold and tried to ignore it or "sleep on it," the issue could have become a full-blown crisis. It certainly would have damaged my reputation.

The lesson is that anyone active online—big or small—should anticipate finding themselves in a crisis situation.

Respond Rapidly with Instant Web Sites

Sometimes when news breaks fast, the best way to ride the wave is to quickly build a new web site.

You may have seen a YouTube video called *Baby Cory Dancing to Beyonce*. This funny clip showing a baby dancing in his diaper became a YouTube sensation, with 10 million views and counting. Cory, just over a year old, was in his grandmother's home in Auckland, New Zealand, when the TV started playing Beyonce's music video "Single Ladies." Cory crawled over, stood, and began to dance. Luckily, his dad Chester had a video camera handy and recorded the whole thing, which he then posted on YouTube.

But it didn't end there.

When Cory's dad realized people around the world were buzzing about the video, and as stories began to appear in media outlets like CNN and *Time*, he quickly created a web site called "Single Babies" where fans could donate to Cory's college fund. He then included a link to the site with the YouTube video, so fans could easily find it. The site has since accepted advertising, and you can even buy T-shirts. All these proceeds also go toward the Cory Elliott Education Fund. Of course, Cory's video spread around the Web in real time as people talked it up on social media, and mainstream media pushed it along even faster. But it was the quick thinking of Cory's dad in creating the "Single Babies" site that snagged all those donations and T-shirt sales while the video was hot.

So when the spotlight suddenly falls on your activities, waste no time! Get your message up fast.

For example, if you run a humanitarian organization that is active in an area suddenly struck by a natural disaster, let the world know that you are in a position to help. Give concerned people an opportunity to donate or volunteer by creating a web site overnight.

In the immediate aftermath of the January 12, 2010, earthquake in Haiti, President Obama asked former presidents George W. Bush and Bill Clinton to lead an effort to raise awareness and solicit funds to support Haitian earthquake survivors. The Clinton Bush Haiti Fund was established on the Web using the domain ClintonBushHaitiFund.org. The new dot-org site was up and running within hours, and before the first day had passed, hundreds of thousands of dollars in donations had flowed in. Within days, the initiative had distributed more than $4 million to aid organizations.

A "dot-org" domain name is an excellent option in this case, because it has an inherent reputation of trust, integrity, and credibility. "Buying a dot-org means companies can benefit from those characteristics instantly," says Lauren Price, brand manager at .ORG, The Public Interest Registry. "Marketers and PR professionals can use a dot-org domain name as a vehicle to educate their communities in times of calm as well as in conflict. It provides a well-recognized platform to neutralize crises, communicate causes, and inform communities." Note that a dot-org domain name is available to anyone, not just nonprofit organizations.

The key here is to get the new site up very quickly, right at the time that people are eager to locate credible information on a breaking issue. This requires that a crisis plan is in place so that it can be implemented when appropriate. Part of that plan should include when and how to establish a standalone site and if a .org registration makes sense.

Imagine if Toyota had created a site within hours of learning about sudden acceleration issues with its cars. As an official clearinghouse for information, this site would have been seen by Toyota customers and the media as a credible source of information, but only if the company had communicated quickly and transparently.

Multiple Communications Channels

Thousands of different online channels now offer routes for you to get the word out to your customers. Which ones are best for you? Look where your customers go and follow them.

As you consider the alternatives, be aware that online popularity waxes and wanes. New services burst on the scene, rise in popularity, and then dwindle—again, following the law of normal distribution. As discussed in Chapter 3, interest starts slowly, builds over time, and then trails off. I find it fascinating to look at how Web-adoption patterns exhibit that same bell-shaped curve. The time scales are *much* longer for adoption curves (typically measured in years) than for breaking news stories (measured in hours).

I spoke about this issue with Andrew Davis, chief strategy officer at Boston-based digital content–creation agency Tippingpoint Labs. Davis has analyzed media adoption over many platforms, including well-known ones like Twitter and Scribd and some relatively unknown services like Amiando, Get-Satisfaction, and Qik. His organization has charted some interesting patterns.

"Our hypothesis is founded on the simple principle that the adoption of any platform (blogging, microblogging, photo sharing, or live video streaming) or content distribution channel (youtube.com, slideshare.com, flickr.com, or twitter.com) can be tracked openly and analyzed to determine where in our life cycle it is," Davis says.

This information is useful because, again and again in social networking, the early adopters tend to have more popularity than late adopters. So being an early participant in a network matters. And participating in the fast-growing services that your customers are using is essential.

According to Davis, the New Media Life Cycle has seven distinct phases:

1. **Experiment**—A new platform or channel offers users a new way to communicate, share, or create content. This phase is characterized by a small group of users constantly adding content (usually of low quality but at high frequency).
2. **Adopt**—A wider audience gives the new medium a try, usually attempting to advance the quality of the content being distributed.

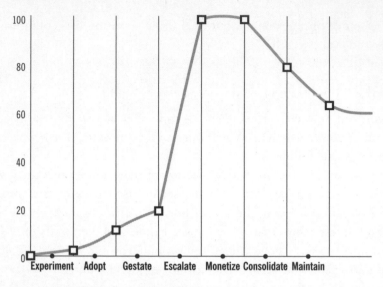

Tippingpoint Labs' Life Cycle Analysis

3. **Gestate**—A small upswing occurs as a core group of early adopters works to understand the value of the medium and provide relevant, frequent, and high-quality content to a wider audience. The gestate phase is where "Internet celebrities" are made on some platforms or channels (such as Tom Dickson, star of the "Will It Blend?" series of YouTube videos).

4. **Escalate**—Rapid growth occurs as users (usually worldwide) begin adding content and contributing frequently. The mass media catches on, and users arrive in large numbers attempting to replicate the success found in the gestation phase. This is frequently the point at which famous people jump in (think Ashton Kutcher on Twitter). The top of the escalation phase spawns a series of copycat channels or platforms each trying to differentiate their offering slightly.

5. **Monetize**—At this point mainstream users start wondering how to measure the ROI (return on investment) of participating in the channel. Companies frequently remain skeptical, wondering how they can profit from the new phenomenon. Growth slows while users try other services and the channel experiments with monetization models.

6. **Consolidate**—When the monetize phase is played out, proving either possible or impossible, attrition rates among user and content creators

are at their highest. Those providing the most valuable content try to find other people like them and build larger communities and audiences for their content. Ironically, it is at this stage that many companies jump into a media platform, because their typically slow and cautious approach prevents them from getting involved earlier.

7. **Maintain**—Finally, the channel enters a maintenance phase having been proven and monetized. The attrition rate approximately balances the adoption rate.

One platform that has gone through all Davis's phases is Second Life, a free, 3-D virtual world where users can socialize, connect, and create, using free voice and text chat. Second Life generated a great deal of interest in 2006 and 2007 because it was one of the first easy-to-use online 3-D worlds. Many companies, including IBM and Reuters, created virtual presences there. Although use has trailed off significantly, Second Life is still the Internet's largest user-created, 3-D virtual world community.

So what this says is that jumping into Second Life now probably won't be the best way to generate attention. There are still people who are active on Second Life, but most of the users have left. And because the service is now shrinking in popularity, media and blogger attention is low.

You will see plots of the relative growth of Second Life based on data from Google Trends as analyzed by TippingpointLabs. Google Trends analyzes a portion of Google Web searches to compute how many searches have been done for each term, relative to the total number of searches done on Google over time. The data is scaled based on the average search traffic of the term you've entered. You can see that Second Life isn't getting too much attention these days.

For an example of a social networking service still in the growth phase as I write this, consider Twitter, a service that has been one of the fastest growing media channels. Launched in late 2006, its first adoption bump came several months later at the South-by-Southwest Interactive Conference in March 2007, when many people began using the service and talking about it to their friends. This bump is barely visible because Twitter has grown so much in the intervening time. The service spiked in popularity in late 2008, just as the mainstream media started to talk it up and famous actors, musicians, and politicians starting gaining publicity using the platform. It's not surprising that the individuals (such as new media strategist Chris Brogan) and

Second Life

Source: Tippingpoint Labs, Google Insights.

companies (like Zappos, JetBlue, and Comcast) who jumped into Twitter during the experiment phase, and who continued to be active during the adoption phase, are now among the most popular people and companies on Twitter.

So the lesson here is that if you want to become well known on a social media site, it's best to find one that is growing quickly but is still in the early stages. "Everyone's looking for the next big viral hit, but trying to manufacture a hit on a platform that's in the escalation phase or later is very difficult," says Andrew Davis. "In the escalation phase, there is a huge volume of users. They're always chasing the latest craze, where everyone's running to make an impact. Trying to break through the noise is very difficult."

Signing on to a service early, in what Davis calls the adoption and gestation phases of the life cycle, is the best way for your content to stand out. Imagine if, just as the entire world is jumping onto Twitter and Facebook and

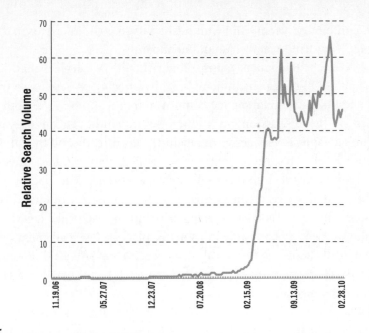

Twitter

Source: Tippingpoint Labs, Google Insight.

struggling to make an impact, you've already been there for several years and have acquired many more followers than your nearest competitor. While the competition is trying to catch up with you, you're already experimenting on other platforms. I do stress experimentation here. It is time-consuming to become active in a new platform, so if it does not grow quickly, there's nothing wrong with abandoning the effort.

Remember, the goal is to connect with your customers. So as you seek out and adopt new platforms, let your customers guide you. Find out what services they're using, and why, to maximize your chances of meeting their needs.

Reaching Fans

If you're really a real-time communicator you're constantly thinking about how you can get the word out in a timely manner.

Toronto-based Celtic-rock jam band Enter the Haggis (ETH) has been recording original music and touring the world for more than a decade. "We've had incredible luck as a band because we attracted fans right from the start who were into our diversity and who pushed us to push ourselves in different directions," says band member Brian Buchanan.

I interviewed Buchanan using CoveritLive!, a service that allowed Buchanan and I to engage in an hour-long, live-text Q&A session so that fans of ETH and people who follow me could watch in real time. (We both spread the word of the discussion on Twitter beforehand.) The live event was Buchanan's idea; he is very active in reaching fans directly and in real time.

Because ETH plays a wide variety of venues, they attract a diverse fan base—which means that no one tool reaches everyone. "Facebook is a different audience than we reach on MySpace, or Twitter, or any of the other social media sites," he says. "There's overlap, sure, but to reach the biggest number of people, we need to be visible in as many places as we can. That's why we try to stay really active on the social networks, but we still send out our email newsletters. There are a ton of people out there who have email addresses but don't use social media."

Buchanan has developed a clever way to update his site and various social-media sites in real time. He has set up automated tools so that when he updates one site (say, the band's Facebook fan page), that update will also appear instantly on the band's site in real time. "I've taken to using some aggregator programs like Ping.fm, where I can post my real-time status updates to all these different places at once," he says. "Facebook we use for instant contests. Like, we'll post a trivia question, and the first person to answer correctly gets a signed copy of an album. Or we'll record a video clip while we're driving in the van and upload the video [via wireless] straight through Facebook onto the front page of the web site. When we post a video, all of a sudden that video is the first thing people see on the front page of the web site."

Another fascinating example of real-time communications from ETH: The band streams their shows live for free on UStream.tv. Before each show, they set up a camera and microphones, connect the system to the Web, and alert fans that a show is on the way.

In a world where most bands (and their management) shun giving away content, here's ETH giving it away as they play it. "I've always been of the mind-set of 'give it away,' like we're giving a calling card . . . and make it the thing that draws people and makes them just part of your community," Buchanan says. "Our band has always been a community. We'll play a festival and 50 people will come from five or six different states, and they'll all meet by a Camp Haggis banner that they put up, and they'll camp together and kind of rally for the band. It's a shared experience of these people, and that seems to be what really draws people in, and what makes them lifelong fans."

Still, giving away your live shows for free and in real time? I wanted Buchanan to tell me more. "I'd rather give away the live stream, and I'd rather a fan go and make 10 copies of our album and give them away, if those things mean we have 10 more fans at shows from then on," he says. "Heads in the crowd are the true measure of success, not chart placements or retail records. If people really want to support you, they'll come to the shows; they'll wear your T-shirts; they'll tell their friends. You can make a living as a touring act without depending on record sales."

Time now to circle back to where this chapter started—and keep in mind what you just read about the enthusiasm and ingenuity Brian Buchanan and Enter the Haggis devote to real-time communication with their customers.

If you work for a large company that still relies on an automated telephone tree as the frontline tool in connecting with customers, this is what I suggest you do. Next time you find yourself in a meeting devoted to choosing new ornaments for the telephone tree, stand up and shout, "Press 9 if you think this is a total waste of time!"

11 Going Mobile, Real Time Is All the Time

You can engage some of the people in real time some of the time. You can engage desktop-computer users when they're at their desks. Sometimes you can engage notebook users at Starbucks. But only when users go mobile can you engage all of the people in real time all of the time. That's why mobile devices are the fastest-growing and most fascinating field in real-time market engagement.

As the rapid proliferation of browser-equipped devices like Blackberry and iPhone puts millions more Americans online all-the-time each year, the United States is catching up with mobile-centric markets like India and Africa. It's true: Mobile Internet connections are more widely used in the rest of the world simply because phones are what people can afford and wireless infrastructure is more reliable than landlines. Even in Japan, a land with last-mile optical fiber that puts the United States to shame, mobile rules because online prime time is the two or more hours people spend riding trains each day.

From here I'll lump together everything from simple handsets to iPhones under the catchall term "mobiles." The really critical distinction is between mobiles with and without GPS (Global Positioning System).

Adding GPS capability to a mobile transforms a general window on the online world into a lens focused on its proximate surroundings. With GPS, a mobile gains awareness of nearby people, objects, and offerings that trumpet their location online. So even in unfamiliar territory, the user is richly informed: "Oh, I see, that's the subway entrance over there, and the post office is next door."

In fact, this is even better than sight as the user can "see through" buildings to identify what's inside or to spot what's on the street behind. Going a step further, as we'll see, this even opens the door to seeing *proposed* buildings from accurate perspectives.

What's more, subject to the user's permission, agents in the proximity can address his or her preferences: "So, we understand you like margaritas," a local bar pops up to say. "Well, it just so happens that half a block away, for the next half hour, margaritas are at half price."

In dynamically competitive, densely packed retail environments like Tokyo, this is going to radically reorder the business hierarchy.

In Tokyo's Roppongi entertainment district you find *several hundred* bars within walking distance of the subway—some visible from the main street, others tucked away on the 14th floor of back-street buildings. To differentiate, many cater to highly refined customer preferences. So if your ideal is to listen to 1930s Danish jazz, drink Mongolian vodka, dress up as a geisha, or play with model trains, your dream bar probably exists in Tokyo. There may even be a bar where you can do all at this the same time. Do not ask me how I know this.

In Roppongi, though, so dense are the offerings that you may be right outside and never know it's there. So once again you settle on Motown, a club visible from the street I used to favor because it had real-time Dow Jones Telerate financial information screens when I was selling an optional service on Dow Jones Telerate.

I'm certain that GPS information is radically altering the hierarchy in Roppongi—and I look forward to confirming this with field research.

This has massive implications for all kinds of businesses worldwide. The ability to contact consumers at the precise moment they're near you and ready to buy exactly what you sell is like some new, god-given power. If you're desperate for business, you can even drop your prices in real time until they relent and come in.

Tapping the World for Recommendations

As someone who finds himself in a new and unfamiliar city almost every month, I love the new "super powers" GPS gives me—especially when I'm hungry. And I'm very particular. If I'm not too hungry, Thai food will do. I'll accept Chinese or Indonesian in a pinch. But when I'm famished—and my wife and daughter say I get mean when I'm hungry—I've gotta have burritos within 10 minutes or I freak out. Until recently, I'd either ask the hotel concierge where to find Thai or Mexican or do a Google search.

Now I go straight to my iPhone and Foursquare or Layar, both of which are GPS-enabled applications that are highly topical about most neighborhoods I stay in.

People use Foursquare, one of the world's fastest-growing social-networking applications, to "check-in" to a featured location and share that information so friends can find them. I find the recommendations that other users give me in each area particularly useful. For example, when I checked in near Boston, the following message popped up: "Since you're so close to Neillio's Gourmet Kitchen, Derek P. says: Get the Bacon Turkey Terrific on focaccia bread." Thanks, Derek. I went for it and it was indeed delicious!

Foursquare is even more useful at large conferences, because you can use it to spot who you didn't realize were there and find where they are hanging out. For example, at South-by-Southwest—March 2010 in Austin, Texas—thousands of people kept up on Foursquare. I would check in at places like the blogger lounge and immediately see which friends were also there. Others used Foursquare to figure out where the best parties were happening, assuming that if many friends were checked in, that had to be the "in" place.

It doesn't take a vivid imagination to picture the marketing implications of all this. Just for starters, if you run a back-street establishment in New York you could divert every visiting techno-cowboy off Fifth Avenue to your door if you got your pitch right. Here are some ways you might go about using Foursquare as a marketing and PR tool:

- **Participate yourself.** To engage your market via Foursquare, all you have to do is participate. Foursquare honors the most frequent visitor to a location as "mayor," a status symbol for the many people who treat Foursquare as a massive game. So if you run the local pizza place, you could check in every day, making yourself mayor. Easy. As mayor of your own establishment, you could offer, say, "mayor specials" to people who checked in for the first time.
- **Cultivate evangelists.** Let someone else become mayor of your pizza place and offer special drink deals when the mayor brings cronies by. When deals like this are attractive, people have been known to compete to oust the incumbent. If several compete for this, each runs up a sizable

tab in the process. And people talk and tweet about being mayor, which builds buzz for the establishment. (Speaking of bragging, I am mayor of Kushboo Indian Restaurant near Boston. See how they get a free plug?)

- **Special offers.** You can also pitch special offers—"Serving free garlic bread to Foursquare users"—to passersby without annoying them. You're not serving spam on that garlic bread because these people are actively looking.
- **Get fans' opinions.** Once you identify your most frequent visitors, involve them in decisions. Ask them how you should change the menu. Get your current "mayor" to devise a "mayor's special."

When I was at South-by-Southwest in Austin, checking into Buffalo Billiards one evening, I was notified that: "Mayor receives 40% off entire tab for one week or until unseated as mayor. 5 check-ins get shot and beer free." I just kept hoping I'd see the first Western-style saloon fistfight over a Foursquare mayoralty.

Looking to Buy a House

Foursquare is good, but at the time of writing (mid-2010), I'm even more obsessed with Layar, an iPhone application I discovered earlier this year in Amsterdam.

Layar is a free mobile application that uses your GPS location to show a layer of real-time information about nearby sites, presented on top of the image shown on your mobile's camera. The founders of Layar call it "augmented reality." I call it cool.

If I'm in a city, I open up the Layar application on my iPhone and look through the iPhone camera. I then add "layars" on top of the image in the camera to superimpose information about whatever restaurants, clubs, real estate for sale, tourist sites, and entertainment venues I see.

So when I'm in the United States and I've got to have Mexican food right now, I open up the "Eat" layar, point the camera at the street, and see various restaurant names and locations pop up as a layer on top of the camera image. (Note that most data providers creating layars are country-specific.)

As I pan the camera around city streets, other nearby restaurants pop into view with a marker on the building. So I keep panning until I find a Mexican joint. Cool stuff.

The people who run Layar have built partnerships with real-time data vendors who supply the content available within the application. Restaurant chains like In-n-Out Burger have a layar. Colleges have created layars with maps that let you navigate their campuses. Next time I'm hungry in Japan (which *will* happen) I will bring up the "Hot Pepper" layer showing restaurants in Tokyo and other major cities.

Think of Layar as a cable TV provider, with your mobile in place of the television. The various content suppliers (there are hundreds) are like the different cable TV stations. Which program each station shows depends on where you are, based on your GPS coordinates.

Funda Real Estate, operator of the largest real-estate portal in the Netherlands, worked with Layar (which is also Dutch) to launch the first real-estate portal on the service. It displays information on just about every property for sale in Holland—typically more than 200,000 listings—attracting nearly 3 million unique visitors each month.

"We project houses for sale onto the Funda layar," says Jeroen Wilhelm, marketing director of Funda Real Estate. "If you look at a street with your naked eye, you may see a couple of houses with 'For Sale' signs outside of the door. But if you look through the camera, the Funda layar shows a dot on each house for sale [not just the ones with signs in front], giving you a real-time layar upon reality."

Click on any dot the Funda real estate layer shows you, and you get full information: price, number of rooms, floor area, and contact information for the listing agent. "People use it on the street, when they look around, and say, 'Hey, this is a nice neighborhood, let's see what's for sale here,'" Wilhelm says. "But there's more. If you're looking for a house, you might also be interested in checking out local shops and restaurants, and you can do that using other layars. This gives you a feel for the neighborhood. It's a big mesh of databases, based on the location of the user, and it brings in a new dynamic."

Wilhelm says that in some markets, 10 to 20 percent of traffic on real estate sites comes through mobile. Funda is investing in mobile marketing now because Wilhelm sees significant growth on the horizon.

Amazingly, Funda is working with Layar to implement a new phase of augmented reality that will let people visualize buildings—with accurate perspective—that are still in the planning stage. A potential buyer looking at a vacant plot of land through the camera would see the future structure superimposed in 3-D on the site. Exciting stuff!

Reaching Buyers via Mobile

Many current mobile devices do not have GPS capability, so the full potential of location-dependent marketing and PR waits in the future. In the meantime there are other ways to harness the power of mobile.

In many countries, people now use mobile-phone cameras as bar code scanners to quickly collect localized information. For example, many display ads on Tokyo subway cars (where more than half the riders seem to be using mobile Internet) feature bar codes. As passengers take photos of these codes, they're taken to mobile web sites that provide more information—and sometimes even discount coupons.

On a recent visit to Japan, I received several business cards that included a bar code, making it simple to download the person's contact information.

Japan is at the forefront of many aspects of mobile marketing. As mentioned, this is partly because quality online time for many Japanese is the many hours they spend riding commuter trains. (Incidentally, this same need to squeeze quality time from a crowded train ride is what spawned the Sony Walkman.)

Speaking of Sony. . . . Sony Pictures Entertainment utilized Mixi, a Japanese social networking service with more than 2 million users, to market the movie *Angels and Demons* in Japan. Since 70 percent of Mixi members access the service via mobiles, Sony Pictures developed an interactive application for mobile devices to promote the movie and get people talking, wherever they were.

Another way to reach buyers via mobile is through SMS ("Short Message Service," aka text messaging). But since nobody wants their text-message stream to get clogged with advertising, intermediaries have popped up.

In the San Francisco area, Mobile Spinach Inc. has developed a service that sends offers and deals to members via text message. The Mobile Spinach twist is that users opt-in to only receive customized offers based on lifestyle choices, preferred categories, and contact preferences (such as frequency of messages). Mobile Spinach focuses on deals from local lifestyle businesses in categories such as shopping, nightlife, events, travel, dining and food, arts and music, and gyms and spas.

"With local information, people really want to dial-in to control their experience," says John Vitti, chief marketing officer of Mobile Spinach. "Someone in San Francisco can sign up and say they want to hear about Italian food, at a certain price point, in a certain neighborhood, on certain dates, and have that sent to their cell phone. It can get that granular. What we're finding is that when you give the user control by making information timely and relevant for them, they then trust the deals and share them. That benefits merchants and users alike."

Pitching to mobile users in real time becomes even more interesting when consumers state detailed preferences and open themselves up to bids. Say you want special deals on wine in San Francisco on Saturday afternoons, restaurant offers on Tuesday and Thursday evenings, or discounts on live performances any time. You put these desires out to tender.

"There is an urgency factor with many offers," Vitti says. "Popular restaurants in San Francisco like Midi, a really high-end French restaurant, and Iman, a famous Peruvian restaurant, might message that they have a few tables open. Or the San Francisco ballet might have extra tickets and discount them on the night of the performance. On the user side, that creates a sense of urgency, because it is a limited time thing so it really brings buyers and sellers together nicely." Because consumers can personalize their offers down to a high level of detail, unwanted messages are kept to a minimum. In my case, I can get offers for Indian and Mexican restaurants on weekday afternoons, but I'm not going to get unwanted burger or sushi messages.

Real-time mobile marketing and PR is in its infancy. But the potential benefits to lifestyle businesses in particular are enormous. As the business models around services like Mobile Spinach, Foursquare, and Layar mature and new services spring up, opportunities abound for any organization selling perishable products like food or performance tickets. The airline industry has been run on dynamic pricing for decades. Now mobile technology allows local businesses to market unsold inventory in real time and maximize revenue.

The power to reach buyers at the time *and place* they're looking for what you offer is the natural next step in online marketing. Watch, the wave is coming.

12 They Want It Immediately

In 2002, I was part of a team that created and launched a new product offering to the financial markets. The product category, corporate earnings call transcripts, already existed. Our twist was to offer the full transcripts *immediately* after the earnings conference call concluded.

As we discuss in this chapter, you can often create a new market niche, and a competitive edge, by delivering *faster* than everybody else, by doing in real time something that normally takes much longer.

My client in 2002 was Fair Disclosure Financial Network Inc. (FDfn), an outfit that transcribes corporate earnings conference calls and makes this information available in real time to subscribers around the world. FDfn had access to quarterly corporate conference calls (in which companies brief analysts and the media on their financial results) because U.S. securities law (Regulation Fair Disclosure) requires publicly traded companies to make earnings conference calls open to the public.

Before FDfn entered the market, there were two less-than-ideal ways to access this information: You could listen in on the conference call live or on tape (via a toll-free number or Webcast connection), or you could wait several days to get a transcript. Both ways had flaws. The calls themselves are long—an hour or more—and many people listening are waiting for specific information, such as commentary on the company's financial outlook over the next year. As dozens of major companies do their calls on the same day, it's almost impossible for one person to catch them all. But waiting days for a transcript means reporters and analysts lose the chance to provide real-time commentary.

> In every industry there is opportunity to do for customers in real time what now takes a long time.

Enter FDfn and the real-time corporate-earnings call-transcript service. FDfn (now part of Thomson Corporation) transcribes thousands of corporate conference calls each quarter using a proprietary technology to produce the transcript as the call is in progress. Humans check each transcript in real time, listening to the call on a slight delay and amending any mistakes in transcription. The finished transcript is usually available within minutes of the call's conclusion. As this real-time product was exactly what the market needed at the time more than 1,000 clients quickly signed up for unlimited access to the transcripts. A new company was born on the strength of a real-time product.

I Want It Now

Instant gratification is a powerful product attribute in the always-on, real-time culture we live in today. Whatever it is, do it faster and you'll win market share. I'd argue that Google's tremendous rise was fueled by its development of a real-time capability for online advertising. Although Google is known for its search engine, the innovation that turned it into one of the most successful companies on the planet is the real-time Google AdWords application, which allows advertisers to bid for ad placement by keyword.

Google was certainly not the first to offer ads on its site. But it revolutionized Web advertising by creating a simple, self-service model that allowed anyone to bid for text-based ad placement in real time.

You've seen these ads that appear alongside your search results on Google. For instance, a real-estate agent in San Diego might want to bid on ads to appear whenever someone searches "San Diego real estate." But this is exactly the phrase every other realtor in San Diego wants, so the price gets bid up. The real-time functionality of Google AdWords enables customers to change bids at any time, helping them manage their ad budgets to reach as many people as possible. This real-time advertising vehicle is immensely popular and generates billions of dollars a year for Google.

> There is room in every market for smart organizations to seize market share and profits by providing service at speed.

Consider your own marketplace. What task could you make real time? Would your buyers be willing to pay a premium to get it faster? Or is there an untapped market waiting for you to deliver in real time?

Real Time with the Grateful Dead

I'm a huge fan of the Grateful Dead, having listened to their music since the first live show I attended in 1979. The Dead were there from the early days of psychedelia in mid-1960s San Francisco. But where other bands fell by the wayside, the Dead have continued to win new fans in each rising generation. Why? As a "Deadhead," my first answer is: "Because the music has no equal." But wearing my suit—and I *don't* have a pony-tail—I have to admit it's because the Grateful Dead are smart marketers.

From the 1970s, the Grateful Dead encouraged concertgoers to record their live shows, establishing "taper sections" where fans' equipment could be set up for the best sound quality. When nearly every other band said "no," the Grateful Dead said "sure," cooperating with a huge network of people who traded tapes in the pre-Internet days.

Thousands of shows from the band's 45-year history have been taped. The Dead always jam and improvise, so each show is different. That means ardent fans may have hundreds of show recordings. The band is happy to have Deadheads (as fans are known) download for free and make copies for friends. Whatever they lose on CD royalties is more than compensated by the continual attraction of new fans to concerts on the band's endless touring schedule.

With the passing of lead singer and guitarist Jerry Garcia in 1995, the band retired the Grateful Dead name for touring. However, they play on in various incarnations including The Dead (all four surviving members plus other musician friends) and most recently as Furthur (bassist Phil Lesh, guitarist Bob Weir, and friends). On recent tours, Furthur has offered fans several inventive real-time product offerings.

On your way into a Furthur concert, or at intermission, you can go to a booth and order a high-quality recording of that very show on CD. And you can pick up your CD immediately after the show is over.

The real-time system works like this. When you order a CD, for about $20, you are given a special wristband to wear. As the show rocks on, the recording crew burns a series of three CDs, finalizing the last one just after the last note is played. The CD crew then works like lightning to duplicate and package the three-CD set as concertgoers file out. Customers then line up to exchange wristbands for recordings. That's about as real time as it comes!

The guy next to me at a recent concert in Worcester, Massachusetts, said he buys the set because he wants to relisten to the show on his three-hour drive back to Vermont. I appreciate the high-quality recording and mixing, which to my ear are superior to the homemade recordings found online.

At each stop on The Dead's 2009 tour, a collectible book featuring the photography of longtime Grateful Dead photographer Jay Blakesberg was also on sale. Each hard-cover collectible book is unique to that particular show. Fans go to Blurb.com to place an order for a book from their show, and it arrives in the mail a few days later. For many fans, a book like this is more interesting than a generic program because it features shots from the actual show they attended.

"The idea for the books started out as a conversation with The Dead management, with Jill Lesh in particular, Phil's wife and manager," Blakesberg told me. "She is a very forward-thinking person, and she wanted photography merchandise of some kind that was more than just a tour book. It's expensive to make tour books because it's inventory that you have to carry. We wanted to do a book that would have photos like an album from each show."

Blakesberg traveled with the band and had full access to create the photos for the books. "I shot intimate moments of these guys on stage and backstage," he says. "I was able to capture those choice moments when nobody else but the band is in the room. It's unique for the band to allow me to document it and then share with the fans, because most people don't get to go backstage. You've got the CD from the show you went to and you've got the book with photos from that show. It's a great memory package."

To promote the availability of the real-time CDs and the instant books, the band distributed postcards to fans. "At every show, we put out a few thousand postcards on cars in the parking lot. They were on all the merchandise tables and flowering the reserved seats on the floor of the venue," Blakesberg says. "Over 20 shows, it was a lot of postcards pointing people to the availability of the books and CDs."

With teams producing both CDs and books in real time you can imagine the intensity of the backstage operation. Blakesberg says it's a huge challenge for both teams, which share facilities on-site. "After the show is over, we upload the photos to The Dead web site and other web sites interested in covering the tour," he says. "Then I do an edit for the book, picking photos and choosing a cover shot for each stop on the tour."

Although the creation of concert-specific books requires considerable speed, the CDs need to be created even faster. "They already have two disks made by the time the show ends, and they do the third as quickly as possible," Blakesberg says. "They had stacks of blank CDs, and these recoding towers would zip and they'd push them all in, hit record, and they'd start going boom, boom, boom. Then the CDs come out and they quickly sleeve them up. Next, they rush these boxes out, 100 CD packages at a time, to the merchandise tables. The first hundred people in line would get them. They'd run back and the next hundred CD packages would be ready. And they would do that over the course of 30 minutes until everybody got their CDs."

The band also released an iPhone application called *The Dead Tour 2009— ALL ACCESS*, which included streaming audio from all the shows on the tour, streaming video, blogs, and photos shot by Blakesberg. Interestingly, as each show was happening, Blakesberg live-tweeted the set lists, so people who were not there could check in real time what songs the band was playing (out of a possible 150 or so songs that the band had rehearsed for this tour). "My tweets went right to the iPhone application, so within seconds you knew what they were playing at that moment," he says. "Phil Lesh and Bob Weir are both very technologically savvy guys. Both are iPhone guys, so they really liked the iPhone app."

The Dead Tour iPhone application was featured in the media, particularly on technology blogs. This demonstrates once again a key idea in this book: Interesting real-time applications attract attention. "We got so much press on it, and that has value," Blakesberg says. "Maybe that sold the band another 5,000 tickets over the course of the tour." At about $45 a ticket, that's nearly

$250,000 in additional revenue, much more than the development costs of an iPhone application.

The Grateful Dead have always used technology in innovative ways and their marketing culture has always stressed openness and availability. So it's not surprising that the band is now experimenting with real-time products. "It's cool that they are still, 45 years into their career, completely cutting edge," Blakesberg says. "Things like the iPhone app keep The Dead in the forefront of technology. But the blitz, the marketing, the awareness of it also makes people think, 'Oh, I want to go see a show.'"

One of the most popular touring bands in history, the surviving members of the Grateful Dead are still interacting with fans in interesting (and real-time) ways, continually driving new fans to the music, keeping the old timers engaged, and ensuring that today's tours still frequently sell out.

For much more on what every business can learn from the most iconic band in history, take a look at my book *Marketing Lessons from the Grateful Dead* which I co-wrote with Brian Halligan, CEO of HubSpot.

Real-Time Products for Your Marketplace

As you consider a real-time product offering in your marketplace, make sure you get out of your comfortable offices and meet with your potential customers. Take the time to discuss what people are willing to pay for to get service in real time. The more research you do, the more likely you are to come up with that unique idea for a successful real-time product that nobody has considered.

> Ask your customers what kind of premium they're willing to pay for real-time service.

In speaking with many businesses that have developed real-time offerings, I've observed that the spark of an idea comes more often from customers than from staff. Insiders are usually too insular to imagine new offerings that provide more than just incremental change.

Say, for example, that a prospective home buyer casually mentions she would like to know when houses sell in the neighborhood. A smart realtor would respond by tweeting real-time sales data.

Hot Jobs in Real Time?

In every market, there's opportunity to strip out time to accomplish tasks much more quickly. Figure out how to do that and you'll hone a competitive edge that wins new customers. But to succeed at this, you need to communicate the advantage you offer.

FedEx remains the gold standard in this regard. They pioneered the overnight delivery business in the early 1970s by outdoing the U.S. Postal Service on guaranteed speed. Even though their rates were more expensive, they attracted millions of customers with the slogan, "Absolutely, Positively Overnight."

FedEx carved a new niche by spotting a problem. It wasn't just that postal service was too slow; customers simply could not depend on the postal delivery standard. They could use a fax machine back then, but fax did not deliver original documents. So customers flocked to a provider that promised to solve real problems.

Recruitment—headhunting—is another business that has historically operated slowly. When an organization has an opening to fill, the process of locating suitable candidates and making a hiring decision frequently takes months. HR departments are typically charged with looking for what's called active talent: people who are actively looking for a job. HR people post positions on their corporate sites, they search resumes in their databases, and they use job boards like Monster. But none of that does anything to find "passive talent," people who have the skills but are happily employed and not looking. So HR people engage headhunters to dig deeper. And positions remain open for months as recruiters work their networks to find the right people.

Hollister Inc., a Massachusetts-based recruiter, aims to deliver what it calls "Recruiting 2.0," an outreach strategy aimed at so-called passive candidates. "We're reaching professionals who are gainfully employed but possess skills hiring companies desire," says Meg Toland, marketing and communications director at Hollister. "We have been successful in reaching candidates who are less likely to frequent job boards and where other staffing agencies simply cannot."

Hollister bypasses the cumbersome and time-consuming phone calls favored by other firms, instead engaging candidates through multiple networking communities on Twitter, LinkedIn, and Facebook. There are communities set up for each area in which Hollister provides recruiting services, including accounting and finance, administration, creative and marketing, technology, sales, and human resources.

"We recognized that nobody wants to be solicited," Toland says. "But everyone has the desire to network, so we launched communities local to Boston. We want people to find, say, the Boston marketing communities on Facebook, LinkedIn, and Twitter."

Hollister's professional networking communities in the Boston area include:

- Facebook: Boston Technology Hub, Boston Creative, Boston Accounting & Finance, Boston HR, and Boston Marketing
- Twitter: @BostonHiring, @BostonTechHub, @AccountingMA, @CreativeBoston, and @BostonMarketing
- LinkedIn: Boston Creative Group, Boston Jobs, Boston Technology Hub, Boston Marketing Group, and Boston HR Leaders
- Blogs: Boston Hiring Blog, Boston Jobs Blog, and Boston Networking Blog

People choose to follow what's happening via the social networking medium of their choice. Each community includes news, information, networking opportunities, industry events, and—of course—job information. Toland and her colleagues at Hollister understand that you build these communities by understanding what each group wants (e.g., marketing professionals in Boston) and delivering it.

Once they create an irresistibly targeted environment, headhunters can target whatever species they're after. The accountants are in this compound, the techies are over there. To see which individuals shine they just have to listen to the conversation.

By developing thriving communities of professionals, each a potentially ideal candidate for a particular job opening, Hollister recruiters are able to act quickly to fill vacancies at client companies. For example, when a client wants candidates immediately, Hollister might post something like "Boston tech hot job" on Twitter and other social media to gain attention. "People click 'hot job' listings quickly," says Toland. "It's like they don't want to miss out. Many will click the link and apply for the job immediately, a very different experience for the job seeker. However, on sites like Monster there are limitations to the number of posts because each job listing costs money. So there isn't a big sense of urgency." Note how the choice of wording ("hot job") informs potential applicants that this is a real-time opportunity to be responded to immediately.

The new model drives many more applicants to the jobs, too. "Our web site traffic averaged 2,500 hits per month in late 2008," Toland says. "With Recruiting 2.0, we have seen a steady monthly increase of measurable qualified traffic. Today our top sources of referring traffic include Twitter, LinkedIn, Facebook, and the Boston Hiring Blog. The numbers are still climbing."

Hollister gets paid by the companies who use their services to find talent. For Hollister clients, getting qualified candidates rapidly (sometimes in just an hour or two) transforms the way companies use recruitment services. "We frequently get people who want to find contract employees immediately," Toland says. "The client needs someone tomorrow. We are working with 24 different social networking communities, so we constantly put the best and hottest jobs in front of people."

For Hollister, real-time considerations revealed a new way to do business in a typically stodgy marketplace.

Book Publisher Goes Real Time with
Truman Fires MacArthur

When President Obama chose to replace General Stanley A. McChrystal in June 2010, following the fallout from the general's controversial comments in a *Rolling Stone* article, the media was in a frenzy. Because McChrystal was the top U.S. commander in Afghanistan, more than 13,000 mainstream media stories and blog posts were written in just a few days.

But what about books? It takes a more than a year to write and publish a book, right? So how can a book author jump into the fray?

A Real-Time E-Book

Two days after the Obama fires McChrystal news broke, book publisher Simon & Schuster released an e-book called *Truman Fires MacArthur* on Amazon Kindle and other e-book services.

Wow—this is an amazing example of real-time product development.

When the entire world is focused on Obama firing McChrystal, a historian provides near-instant context by releasing information on how Truman fired MacArthur.

The *Truman Fires MacArthur* e-book was developed in real time as an excerpt from the 1992 book *Truman* by David McCullough.

Publisher Simon & Schuster took the related content from the full-length book, created the e-book, slapped on an ISBN, and was selling it electronically within 48 hours of the news breaking.

Real-Time Futures Trading Training Course

Today, it is big business to offer training courses online. In the financial markets, much of the action centers on learning how to make money day-trading from home: stocks, bonds, commodities, futures—you name it, there's a course for you.

Richard Regan, managing partner of Pro Trading Course, developed a training program that is completely different from that of all his competitors. Regan works from the floor of the CME Group in Chicago, one of the last open outcry marketplaces. Here, traders still work in the pits, buying and selling with hand signals. At the same time, though, anybody can buy and sell electronically; the CME Group is also the largest electronic exchange in America. "We trade electronically, but we also have all the pits right here in front of us, all the charts so that we know exactly what's going on in the market, and what we're buying and what we're selling," Regan told me when I visited him on the trading floor.

Regan developed Pro Trading Course, a real-time online virtual trading-room service for up-to-the second instruction on trading in the futures markets. Traders follow along on the actual screens Regan is using and hear him explain via streaming audio as he makes trades live from the CME Group floor. The service is sold as a subscription for $499 per month and has seen steady growth of about 25 new clients each month.

"We're the only ones actually approved by the CME Group on the floor to provide this real-time news service, real-time trading tips, and coaching," Regan says.

Subscribers see in real time the same trading screens that Regan uses to make futures trades. "I wear a headset so they can hear exactly what I'm doing. I talk through all my trades, what I'm buying, what I'm selling, and you can hear everything I'm actually doing in real time. I'll see any news stories here on Twitter or on my live news services, and I then disseminate them to subscribers and figure out how we're going to make a trade decision based on that." Regan says it is like a reality TV show. He does his trading job and people who are subscribed to the Pro Trading Course service see everything he's seeing and hear everything he's saying, all in real time.

Regan also uses real-time techniques to market his Pro Trading Course online. He uses his Twitter feed to share free market tips that also serve to promote his service. In fact, he is one of the few people tweeting live from the floor of the CME Group. "During the day, as much as I can, time permitting, I'll put posts on Twitter about what I'm buying or selling or what's going on in the market," he says. "As people comb through the fire hose of information on Twitter, they find these things that I've posted. If they like it, they may end up going to our web site."

He also uses Twitter as a way to connect one on one with potential subscribers. "Twitter has provided the opportunity for people to connect to people that before were unattainable. I'll have somebody from Nebraska send me a message asking about the market today, and I will answer it. We probably drive about 1,000 hits per month to our site just through Twitter, and some of those people are converting to paid subscribers."

In a crowded market that offers literally thousands of ways to learn about futures trading, Regan pioneered a real-time approach. And his clients love it. I watched him in action one morning and saw many "thank you" messages pour in as he explained a trade that made people money in real time. As a result, Regan's business is growing quickly.

I'm not going to tell you what the opportunity is for you. I'll leave that to your imagination. But look around. In almost every field of endeavor there's an opportunity to harness speed to your advantage and create a product or even an entire company from it.

Grow Your Business Now

In Part Three, we move beyond tactical approaches to reaching customers and the media in real time to look at how you can transform your organization to function in real time.

The process starts with your people. Encourage everyone on the team to actively communicate. Give them confidence by giving each individual leeway within clear guidelines.

Once your people are on board, transform your online interface—web site, blogs, and other tools—into a real-time machine.

Above all, this is about a mind-set that has to start at the top. If your leaders get the need for real-time speed, they must give explicit permission and proactively advocate cultural change at all levels.

13 Let Them Communicate . . . *Now*

All these new communications tools are *so* disruptive and unsettling. They make those busybodies in every workplace who take it upon themselves to look over the shoulders of others feel like—gasp!—they're losing control. That's why a debate is in progress at companies worldwide. What types of communications should people be allowed or perhaps encouraged to do at work?

One side of the debate—usually led by HR and legal counsel—insists new forms of communications are frivolous at best and dangerous at worst. Fearing they might lose control these people prefer to clamp down on the use of social media at work.

To be fair, I do understand *part* of the argument here—anything employees say on social media can be seen instantly by the entire world—and that can be a scary prospect. Remember the pizza guy who stuffed cheese up his nose.

All sorts of things can go wrong in an age when one of your salespeople—after three martinis—can tweet insults to a *New York Times* reporter from his barstool. And when your potential business partner can see, on Foursquare, just how many bars you've been to this week. Given what can happen, no wonder people fret that we're going a bit loosey-goosey on the real-time communications front.

Then again, we've been through all this before. Where I worked in the late 1980s, company officials debated the wisdom of providing PCs and email addresses to staff. In the end, the bosses decided that only those at director-level could have email address, because the peons might "give away company secrets." And besides, they reasoned, why would rank-and-file employees need email anyway? Isn't that what the phone and fax are for?

Of course, this silliness broke down as email became ubiquitous. Today, even in info-uptight China office workers have access to computers and email.

So why today are we hearing the *exact same arguments* used to justify preventing employees from communicating in real time?

Based on informal surveys (shows of hands at my corporate speaking engagements), I estimate that 25 percent of large organizations block employee access to online social media. An even higher percentage forbids employees to comment on blogs, forums, and chat rooms as part of their jobs.

In doing so, these organizations actively put up roadblocks to stop employees from engaging in real time. On an evolutionary ladder leading to the kind of enlightened real-time corporate culture this book advocates, this must surely rank as Neanderthal.

> To engage your marketplace right now, free your people to communicate in real time.

Here are some common reasons why companies prohibit real-time communications:

- People may say something inappropriate and harm the company's reputation: "What if a junior employee gives away a trade secret?"
- Twitter is just inane chitchat—no serious business happens there: "Who cares what you had for lunch?"
- If people are online, it will take too much of their time: "When will they be able to do actual work?"

Bottom line: Sure, huge new fields of potential for disaster have opened up in recent years—and they are not going away again, *ever*. So you will never succeed in stamping it out with prohibition. More likely, you will succeed in this new era with a communications regime that embraces reality, fosters engagement, and leads to sustainable growth. Throughout this book, we have seen people succeeding at this.

For large outfits, the key to overcoming this challenge starts with a realistic, easy to understand and apply set of real-time communications guidelines.

Real-Time Communications Policy

Develop an effective code of real-time communications and proactively embed it throughout your organization. Train it, demonstrate it, discuss it, and review it until this becomes second nature to everyone. Have your people internalize it as deeply as the instincts that tell them when it's safe to turn left at a traffic light (or right if they're Brits). This is fully possible.

IBM, Telstra, and the U.S. Air Force are among large organizations worldwide that made huge strides by creating formal guidelines for employees. To make them accessible, all three employers publish their guidelines online so anyone can see.

IBM's code is called *Social Computing Guidelines*. The USAF has *New Media and the Air Force*. The purpose of both is the same: to provide rules to help employees engage the marketplace and customers in real time—effectively and responsibly.

The IBM guidelines include all manner of helpful instructions. Be who you are; be thoughtful about how you present yourself in online social networks; respect copyright and fair use laws; protect confidential and proprietary information; add value; don't pick fights; and don't forget your day job. But the single most important guideline in the IBM document is this: Speak in the first-person singular. In fact, I think that speaking in the first-person singular is essential to understanding what we're really talking about here.

When somebody from your company says something in a social network using "we" (as in "We're going to create a new product and release it in December!"), readers might think that this is some sort of formal corporate announcement, even if the person is not authorized to talk about product launches. However, when the same employee uses the first-person singular (e.g., "I'm working on a new product targeted for December release!") it becomes a personal statement. Simple and clear.

Included in the following section in its entirety is the IBM guidelines document. Please do take the time to read it; there are many essential lessons to learn here, and space prohibits me from following up on each one of them explicitly.

IBM Social Computing Guidelines

Blogs, Wikis, Social Networks, Virtual Worlds, and Social Media

In the spring of 2005, IBMers used a wiki to create a set of guidelines for all IBMers who wanted to blog. These guidelines aimed to provide helpful, practical advice—and also to protect both IBM bloggers and IBM itself, as the company sought to embrace the blogosphere. Since then, many new forms of social media have emerged. So we turned to IBMers again to re-examine our guidelines and determine what needed to be modified. The effort has broadened the scope of the existing guidelines to include all forms of social computing.

Below are the current and official "IBM Social Computing Guidelines," which continue to evolve as new technologies and social networking tools become available.

Have you seen social computing behavior or content that is not in keeping with these guidelines? Report inappropriate content via email.

Introduction

Responsible Engagement in Innovation and Dialogue

Whether or not an IBMer chooses to create or participate in a blog, wiki, online social network or any other form of online publishing or discussion is his or her own decision. However, emerging online collaboration platforms are fundamentally changing the way IBMers work and engage with each other, clients and partners.

IBM is increasingly exploring how online discourse through social computing can empower IBMers as global professionals, innovators and citizens. These individual interactions represent a new model: not mass communications, but masses of communicators.

Therefore, it is very much in IBM's interest—and, we believe, in each IBMer's own—to be aware of and participate in this sphere of information, interaction and idea exchange:

To learn: As an innovation-based company, we believe in the importance of open exchange and learning—between IBM and its clients, and among the many constituents of our emerging business and societal ecosystem. The rapidly growing phenomenon of user-generated web content—blogging, social web-applications and networking—are emerging important arenas for that kind of engagement and learning.

To contribute: IBM—as a business, as an innovator and as a corporate citizen—makes important contributions to the world, to the future of business and technology, and to public dialogue on a broad range of societal issues. As our business activities increasingly focus on the provision of transformational insight and high-value innovation—whether to business clients or those in the public, educational or health sectors—it becomes increasingly important for IBM and IBMers to share with the world the exciting things we're learning and doing, and to learn from others.

In 1997, IBM recommended that its employees get out onto the Internet—at a time when many companies were seeking to restrict their employees' Internet access. In 2005, the company made a strategic decision to embrace the blogosphere and to encourage IBMers to participate. We continue to advocate IBMers' responsible involvement today in this rapidly growing space of relationship, learning and collaboration.

IBM Social Computing Guidelines: Executive Summary

1. Know and follow IBM's Business Conduct Guidelines.
2. IBMers are personally responsible for the content they publish on blogs, wikis or any other form of user-generated media. Be mindful that what you publish will be public for a long time—protect your privacy.
3. Identify yourself—name and, when relevant, role at IBM—when you discuss IBM or IBM-related matters. And write in the first person. You must make it clear that you are speaking for yourself and not on behalf of IBM.
4. If you publish content to any website outside of IBM and it has something to do with work you do or subjects associated with IBM, use a disclaimer such as this: "The postings
(continued)

(*continued*)

on this site are my own and don't necessarily represent IBM's positions, strategies or opinions."

5. Respect copyright, fair use and financial disclosure laws.

6. Don't provide IBM's or another's confidential or other proprietary information. Ask permission to publish or report on conversations that are meant to be private or internal to IBM.

7. Don't cite or reference clients, partners or suppliers without their approval. When you do make a reference, where possible link back to the source.

8. Respect your audience. Don't use ethnic slurs, personal insults, obscenity, or engage in any conduct that would not be acceptable in IBM's workplace. You should also show proper consideration for others' privacy and for topics that may be considered objectionable or inflammatory—such as politics and religion.

9. Find out who else is blogging or publishing on the topic, and cite them.

10. Be aware of your association with IBM in online social networks. If you identify yourself as an IBMer, ensure your profile and related content is consistent with how you wish to present yourself with colleagues and clients.

11. Don't pick fights, be the first to correct your own mistakes, and don't alter previous posts without indicating that you have done so.

12. Try to add value. Provide worthwhile information and perspective. IBM's brand is best represented by its people and what you publish may reflect on IBM's brand.

IBM Social Computing Guidelines: Detailed Discussion

The IBM Business Conduct Guidelines and laws provide the foundation for IBM's policies and guidelines for blogs and social computing. The same principles and guidelines that apply to IBMers' activities in general, as found in the IBM Business Conduct Guidelines, apply to IBMers' activities online. This includes forms of online publishing and discussion, including blogs, wikis, file-sharing, user-generated video and audio, virtual worlds and social networks.

As outlined in the Business Conduct Guidelines, IBM fully respects the legal rights of our employees in all countries in which we operate. In general, what you do on your own time is your affair. However, activities in or outside of work that affect your IBM job performance, the performance of others, or IBM's business interests are a proper focus for company policy.

IBM supports open dialogue and the exchange of ideas. IBM regards blogs and other forms of online discourse as primarily a form of communication and relationship among individuals. When the company wishes to communicate publicly as a company—whether to the marketplace or to the general public—it has well established means to do so. Only those officially designated by IBM have the authorization to speak on behalf of the company.

However, IBM believes in dialogue among IBMers and with our partners, clients, members of the many communities in which we participate and the general public. Such dialogue is inherent in our business model of innovation, and in our commitment to the development of open standards. We believe that IBMers can both derive and provide important benefits from exchanges of perspective.

One of IBMers' core values is "trust and personal responsibility in all relationships." As a company, IBM trusts—and expects—IBMers to exercise personal responsibility whenever they participate in social media. This includes not violating the trust of those with whom they are engaging. IBMers should not use these media for covert marketing or public relations. If and when members of IBM's Communications, Marketing, Sales or other functions engaged in advocacy for the company have the authorization to participate in social media, they should identify themselves as such.

What does an IBMer's personal responsibility mean in online social media activities? Online social media enables individuals to share their insights, express their opinions and share information within the context of a globally distributed conversation. Each tool and medium has proper and improper uses. While IBM encourages

(continued)

(continued)

all of its employees to join a global conversation, it is important for IBMers who choose to do so to understand what is recommended, expected and required when they discuss IBM-related topics, whether at work or on their own time.

Know the IBM Business Conduct Guidelines. If you have any confusion about whether you ought to publish something online, chances are the BCGs will resolve it. Pay particular attention to what the BCGs have to say about proprietary information, about avoiding misrepresentation and about competing in the field. If, after checking the BCG's, you are still unclear as to the propriety of a post, it is best to refrain and seek the advice of management.

Be who you are. Some bloggers work anonymously, using pseudonyms or false screen names. IBM discourages that in blogs, wikis or other forms of online participation that relate to IBM, our business or issues with which the company is engaged. We believe in transparency and honesty. If you are blogging about your work for IBM, we encourage you to use your real name, be clear who you are, and identify that you work for IBM. Nothing gains you more notice in the online social media environment than honesty—or dishonesty. If you have a vested interest in something you are discussing, be the first to point it out. But also be smart about protecting yourself and your privacy. What you publish will be around for a long time, so consider the content carefully and also be judicious in disclosing personal details.

Be thoughtful about how you present yourself in online social networks. The lines between public and private, personal and professional are blurred in online social networks. By virtue of identifying yourself as an IBMer within a social network, you are now connected to your colleagues, managers and even IBM's clients. You should ensure that content associated with you is consistent with your work at IBM. If you have joined IBM recently, be sure to update your social profiles to reflect IBM's guidelines.

Speak in the first person. Use your own voice; bring your own personality to the forefront; say what is on your mind.

Use a disclaimer. Whether you publish to a blog or some other form of social media, make it clear that what you say there is representative of your views and opinions and not necessarily the views and opinions of IBM. At a minimum in your own blog, you should include the following standard disclaimer: "The postings on this site are my own and don't necessarily represent IBM's positions, strategies or opinions."

Managers and executives take note: This standard disclaimer does not by itself exempt IBM managers and executives from a special responsibility when blogging. By virtue of their position, they must consider whether personal thoughts they publish may be misunderstood as expressing IBM positions. And a manager should assume that his or her team will read what is written. A public blog is not the place to communicate IBM policies to IBM employees.

Respect copyright and fair use laws. For IBM's protection and well as your own, it is critical that you show proper respect for the laws governing copyright and fair use of copyrighted material owned by others, including IBM's own copyrights and brands. You should never quote more than short excerpts of someone else's work. And it is good general blogging practice to link to others' work. Keep in mind that laws will be different depending on where you live and work.

Protecting confidential and proprietary information. Social computing blurs many of the traditional boundaries between internal and external communications. Be thoughtful about what you publish—particularly on external platforms. You must make sure you do not disclose or use IBM confidential or proprietary information or that of any other person or company in any online social computing platform. For example, ask permission before posting someone's picture in a social network or publishing in a blog a conversation that was meant to be private.

IBM's business performance. You must not comment on confidential IBM financial information such as IBM's future business performance, business plans, or prospects anywhere in world. This

(continued)

(*continued*)

includes statements about an upcoming quarter or future periods or information about alliances, and applies to anyone including conversations with Wall Street analysts, press or other third parties (including friends). IBM policy is not to comment on rumors in any way. You should merely say, "no comment" to rumors. Do not deny or affirm them—or suggest either denial or affirmation in subtle ways.

Protect IBM's clients, business partners and suppliers. Clients, partners or suppliers should not be cited or obviously referenced without their approval. Externally, never identify a client, partner or supplier by name without permission and never discuss confidential details of a client engagement. Internal social computing platforms permit suppliers and business partners to participate so be sensitive to who will see your content. If a client hasn't given explicit permission for their name to be used, think carefully about the content you're going to publish on any internal social media and get the appropriate permission where necessary.

It is acceptable to discuss general details about kinds of projects and to use non-identifying pseudonyms for a client (e.g., Client 123) so long as the information provided does not make it easy for someone to identify the client or violate any non-disclosure or intellectual property agreements that may be in place with the client. Furthermore, your blog or online social network is not the place to conduct confidential business with a client.

Respect your audience and your coworkers. Remember that IBM is a global organization whose employees and clients reflect a diverse set of customs, values and points of view. Don't be afraid to be yourself, but do so respectfully. This includes not only the obvious (no ethnic slurs, personal insults, obscenity, etc.) but also proper consideration of privacy and of topics that may be considered objectionable or inflammatory—such as politics and religion. For example, if your blog is hosted on an IBM-owned property, avoid these topics and focus on subjects that are business-related. If your blog is self-hosted, use your best judgment and be sure to make it clear that the views and opinions expressed are yours alone and do not represent the official views of IBM. Further, blogs, wikis, virtual worlds, social networks, or other tools hosted outside of IBM's protected Intranet environment should not be used for internal communications among fellow employees. It is fine for IBMers to disagree, but please don't use your external blog or other online social media to air your differences in an inappropriate manner.

Add value. IBM's brand is best represented by its people and everything you publish reflects upon it. Blogs and social networks that are hosted on IBM-owned domains should be used in a way that adds value to IBM's business. If it helps you, your coworkers, our clients or our partners to do their jobs and solve problems; if it helps to improve knowledge or skills; if it contributes directly or indirectly to the improvement of IBM's products, processes and policies; if it builds a sense of community; or if it helps to promote IBM's Values, then it is adding value. Though not directly business-related, background information you choose to share about yourself, such as information about your family or personal interests, may be useful in helping establish a relationship between you and your readers, but it is entirely your choice whether to share this information.

Don't pick fights. When you see misrepresentations made about IBM by media, analysts or by other bloggers, you may certainly use your blog—or join someone else's to point that out. Always do so with respect, stick to the facts and identify your appropriate affiliation to IBM. Also, if you speak about a competitor, you must make sure that what you say is factual and that it does not disparage the competitor. Avoid unnecessary or unproductive arguments. Brawls may earn traffic, but nobody wins in the end. Don't try to settle scores or goad competitors or others into inflammatory debates. Here and in other areas of public discussion, make sure that what you are saying is factually correct.

Be the first to respond to your own mistakes. If you make an error, be up front about your mistake and correct it quickly. In a blog, if you choose to modify an earlier post, make it clear that you have done so.

(continued)

(*continued*)

Use your best judgment. Remember that there are always consequences to what you publish. If you're about to publish something that makes you even the slightest bit uncomfortable, review
the suggestions above and think about why that is. If you're still
unsure, and it is related to IBM business, feel free to discuss it with
your manager. Ultimately, however, you have sole responsibility for
what you post to your blog or publish in any form of online social
media.

Don't forget your day job. You should make sure that your online
activities do not interfere with your job or commitments to
customers.

The IBM guidelines most interest me where they talk about how today's
real-time tools have changed communication; that, plus the way this document encourages IBM employees to embrace the changes. This section really
got my attention:

Emerging online collaboration platforms are fundamentally changing
the way IBMers work and engage with each other, clients and partners.
IBM is increasingly exploring how online discourse through social computing can empower IBMers as global professionals, innovators and citizens. These individual interactions represent a new model: not mass
communications, but masses of communicators. Therefore, it is very
much in IBM's interest—and, we believe, in each IBMer's own—to be
aware of and participate in this sphere of information, interaction and
idea exchange.

On an evolutionary scale ranking those who prohibit real-time engagement as Neanderthal, IBM stands at the top. This is about as evolved and
enlightened as it gets. Bravo, IBM! Here's hoping others follow your example.

Where did IBM get this stuff? How did they put it together? As soon as I
read the guidelines I had to find out.

"The guidelines were created by key contributors to social networking,
such as bloggers, people who do video, and social networkers," says Tim

Washer, head of social-media productions for IBM worldwide. Washer was part of the team that developed the document. "Once we came up with the guidelines, we then ran it by the legal and HR people. We got the initial blogger guidelines agreed to by HR and legal within 48 hours. That's amazing and says a lot about how important it is to let IBMers get out and communicate with the world."

Before the *Social Computing Guidelines*, IBM already had *Business Conduct Guidelines*, a code of conduct that all 400,000 IBM employees use for dealing with ethical quandaries and other matters of professional behavior. For instance, many IBM employees create patented technology and proprietary information, so rules about disclosing inside information had already been addressed in the IBM *Business Conduct Guidelines*. That made developing the guidelines for real-time communication easier, because it was a follow-on document.

"IBM wants IBMers to communicate," Washer says. "A big part of being engaged in the community is feeling comfortable with what you can say and what you can't say, so we wanted to establish the boundaries. If you identify yourself as an IBMer, then you need to adhere to the guidelines. The guidance we offer is that, if you give perspective on a topic that has something to do with IBM, we want you to speak as an IBMer."

How to Develop Real-Time Communications Guidelines

You don't have to work in a 400,000-person company like IBM to benefit from real-time communications guidelines. I think any organization (even one with just a dozen people) should have a set of guidelines in place. Guidelines mean employees know they have the freedom to communicate in real time when the opportunity arises. So here is a set of eight steps to create and implement guidelines for your organization:

1. Get initial agreement from stakeholders (senior executives, HR, PR, legal, etc.) that such guidelines are required. Explain the importance of communicating in real time and the need for comprehensive rules governing what can be done at work. Coming to this initial understanding should win you the authority to actually draft the guidelines.

2. Select a team of about six people to draft the guidelines. Find people who are active communicators from different areas of the company.

3. Study any relevant corporate guidelines already in place (e.g., employee handbook) as IBM had with its *Business Conduct Guidelines*. Many of the issues to be addressed may already be covered by the guidelines. In other cases, there may be policies that contradict what you want to do (such as some companies' prohibitions on communicating online without prior vetting from legal, which kills the speed element). Some existing policies may need to be amended.

4. In creating your guidelines, closely study IBM's *Social Computing Guidelines*, *New Media and the Air Force*, and others like these. Adapt them for your regulatory environment, corporate culture, and marketplace.

5. Share your draft guidelines with stakeholders (listed earlier) and get their sign-offs. If you started with sufficient up-front buy-in (see Step 1) this should go smoothly.

6. Incorporate feedback without getting bogged down by process. You don't want the project to die from endless editing.

7. Publish the guidelines on internal sites, and if you can, externally, the way IBM and the USAF have.

8. Communicate the guidelines to everyone in your organization until it becomes second nature.

Publishing Your Guidelines

Telstra, Australia's largest telecom company, is another organization that created real-time communications guidelines and published them for all to see. *Telstra's 3Rs of Social Media Engagement* talks about real-time communication in terms of three basic principles: representation, responsibility, and respect. The *3Rs* document is presented in a comic-book format—certainly an engaging approach to delivering information to employees. Making these guidelines publicly available shows that the company believes in real-time engagement and wants its constituents to know it.

I was intrigued by the way that Telstra chose to get the word out about the guidelines to more than 40,000 worldwide employees. Not only was the document itself published in comic book format, a module on the *3Rs* was included in the video the company uses for staff training. A short introductory clip of the training video is even published on YouTube for anybody to see.

Telstra's experience shows it is not enough to just publish the guidelines as "shelfware." Employees have to internalize the rules to the point that even when overtired and grumpy they stop themselves from crossing the lines. Creating interesting ways to get the message home is worth the effort.

Encouraging Communications

The British government has also published guidelines encouraging the use of real-time communication among civil servants. I had an opportunity to discuss the guidelines with John Suffolk, chief information officer of Her Majesty's Government.

"It says, get out there and blog," he summarizes. The guidelines say to treat people with respect and to recognize that your words can be interpreted quite differently from your intention. It also cautions bureaucrats against commenting on policy being drafted. "You should only blog about things that are already in the public domain or are signed off by government having gone through the proper parliamentary channels."

Suffolk cited Members of Parliament and government officials who are active on Twitter and using other social networking tools. "We are not saying you must use every single tool, what we are saying is [to] use tools that are appropriate for you, [tools] which will help you engage with citizens and understand what their needs are, because that helps you design better policy."

A fascinating use of government real-time engagement is that many strategy and policy documents are open to public comment, using social tools, as they are being drafted. "For example, I published the government ICT [Information and Communication Technology] Strategy three weeks ago. It's all right to reply, by paragraph," Suffolk says. "You can go in and comment on every single paragraph on that strategy. We are really happy to take views from around the world in terms of what they think about all this."

Soliciting real-time citizen comments on policies that affect their lives is, to my mind, the start of a positive trend. I look forward to seeing other governments around the world follow Britain's lead in real-time democracy.

When One of the Flock Strays

H&R Block has been actively communicating on social networks since 2007. The tax-preparation specialist has a "social-media policy" in place and launched a social-media outreach team in the 2009 tax season.

"Our Client Services organization, with guidance from our Social Media Team, are actively responding to customer service questions, issues, and comments via Twitter, Facebook, and other social networking sites," Zena Weist, director, social media at H&R Block told me.

"Our Ah-ha! moment came the morning after Tax Day [April 15, 2010]," Weist says. "An H&R Block client services associate, who I'll call Joe, went rogue on Twitter. He was 'just having fun' trying to stir up his co-workers by asking his followers to contact him directly through the call center number. What Joe didn't realize was the impact of his tweets. People searching online for H&R Block help came across his 'just for fun' tweets in their search results."

Because Weist and her social-media team actively monitor tax-related comments online, they knew the moment Joe began posting. "What Joe didn't realize was that we had a team monitoring and responding to customer-service inquiries on social networks," she says. "Within 10 minutes, our social-media outreach team had identified and contacted Joe and his manager. About an hour later, Joe had deleted his tweets."

So what was the Ah-ha moment for Weist's team? "We were focusing on communicating with our clients and forgot to update all our associates. Of course, we had covered our bases when we launched our social-media policy—we'd given all our associates access to it and it was easy to reference via our intranet. We had discussed our client services social-media outreach team launch with core teams. What we didn't focus on was 'What's In It For Me' (WIIFM) to all associates."

That afternoon Weist quickly sent an email to all H&R Block associates. It explained that the social-media team was actively listening online; how the client-service outreach team was handling online inquiries; and how all this affected the associates.

An important aspect of having real-time communications guidelines in place is making certain that employees know about the guidelines, understand them, and follow them. When somebody strays, like "Joe" at H&R

Block, it is critical to follow up immediately. In Joe's case, it was a mistake with no malice involved. He apologized and important lessons were learned by all involved. However, in more severe cases, your HR people may need to get involved and disciplinary action taken as required.

Chief Real-Time Communications Officer

I believe so much in the importance of real-time communication that I've got a major proposal to recommend here: Create a new senior position called "chief real-time communications officer."

I see a legitimate need for a high-level individual across a broad range of companies. In larger businesses, this person would be backed by a team of "real-time communications administrators." The challenge is equivalent to similar inflection points that led to the creation of chief information officers in the late 1980s and Webmasters in the 1990s.

This real-time communications role would come with responsibility to provide leadership and coordination for a range of real-time activities, starting with the creation of company guidelines. It would include a mandate to ensure compliance and consistency with those guidelines, once established.

In my travels, I have met many executives who struggle with figuring out how to implement real-time communication across their organizations. The consistency and leadership provided by the person in this new role could help to reduce much of the anxiety around these practices. In larger organizations, there may be too much work for just one person, so a team of people may be more appropriate.

Let me comment for a moment on the actual job title. Some organizations have hired "social-media administrators" or "social-media strategists." Although these job descriptions play roles similar to those I propose, I think the choice of title is significant. Appointing a chief real-time communications officer acknowledges that while social media are *tools,* "real-time communication" is a mind-set. That mind-set is the critical piece.

Reaction to this proposal has been encouraging so far. When I began to explore these ideas on my blog in September 2009, people from as far away as Australia and South Africa joined the conversation.

Together we crowdsourced what the role should look like. Here's what my readers and I came up with:

Real-Time Communication Job Description

- Serve as central coordination point across departments for real-time communication strategy and tactics.
- Be aware of legal, regulatory, and compliance issues within the organizational structure—copyright and intellectual property issues, for example.
- Disseminate knowledge of real-time communication tools, techniques, and philosophies.
- Act as primary contact point and clearinghouse for breaking issues affecting the organization on mainstream or social media.
- Ensure consistency of company presence in social media—in branding, update frequency, and permissions.
- Watch for rogue sites springing up using company branding. Initiate action to delete as appropriate.
- Provide advice on social-media analysis and monitoring and on measurement tools. Ensure appropriate tools are chosen and properly implemented.
- Ensure that the company monitors and responds to appropriate forums in real time.
- Fill key roles in crisis communication planning and execution.
- Advise, train, coach, and counsel other employees on real-time communication.
- Work closely with staff operating corporate web sites to ensure real-time components are implemented.
- Lead efforts to publish and distribute real-time communication guidelines.
- Maintain a list of employees' work-related personal blogs and make available to the public on the company web site.
- Be able to work in a cross-functional, cross-cultural environment.

So where does the real-time communication team report? At IBM and the U.S. Air Force, guidelines were created and are maintained in the communication (public affairs) departments. Some say the real-time communications team should be an IT role, but I think it best fits in PR or marketing. No matter where it sits, the people hired into these roles must have a deep understanding of how modern communication works.

Let Employees Communicate Now

Once you've got guidelines and a real-time communication team in place, give them enough independent authority to get on with the job! If you've done the job right, your real-time team should not need to run to legal every time someone plans to make a blog post. If a company trusts its employees and understands that real-time communication is an important aspect of business today, then it is the lawyers' job to create an environment where that can happen.

It's quite likely that many of your people are already active in social media, never mentioning where they work. Once given permission to communicate actively, freely, and in real time, people will be excited to engage with the marketplace! You may be surprised by what they achieve.

14 How Your Web Site Becomes a Real-Time Machine

So ubiquitous have web sites become that it's hard to believe they've been with us for fewer than 20 years. It was the 1994 introduction of the browser-enabled World Wide Web that gave birth to the web site. Since then they have gone through about four stages of evolution:

1. Early on, web sites were just "brochure-ware," online versions of sales catalogs, corporate profiles, annual reports, and other print collateral.
2. Once people realized they could add more content without running up a huge printer's bill, from 1997 online publishing proliferated in the "Content is King" era.
3. Around the turn of the millennium, as search engines became the primary means of accessing online information, businesses focused on "search engine optimization strategies" to drive traffic to their sites.
4. As consumers learned to use search engines as powerful research tools they naturally began to reward companies who thought like publishers of information, not advertisers of products. I wrote about this new way of doing business in my 2007 book *The New Rules of Marketing & PR*.

Now, we're entering a fifth era of the evolution: transformation of the web site into a real-time marketing (and sales) machine. This is the natural evolutionary outcome of a process that started with a new way to slip brochures under people's doors.

We are arriving at a place where online presence is tangibly *alive*. Like walking into a physical retail space, you immediately encounter real people. They welcome you and greet you by name, or introduce themselves. If you ask a question, they respond right away and in context—not with a list of FAQs. From there, you may quietly browse the shelves and make your purchase—without lining up or talking with staff. But the moment you look puzzled, an insightful shop assistant rushes over to offer help.

We all know what to expect in a real-time retail experience—we get it every day at bricks-and-mortar outlets. I get impatient if I have to wait more than a few minutes for help from a sales clerk (when I want it). And I get annoyed when I'm just browsing and a sales clerk insists on badgering me. But when I have a query and the clerk responded to my question with a list of FAQs, I'd walk out never to return.

Until now, consumers have been so amazed by the research power of the online experience that they've tolerated robotic answers and snail-mail response times. Inevitably, though, expectations will ratchet up not down. And that makes real time an inevitable standard that your site must match sooner than later.

> Consumers' online expectations are ratcheting up. Just as no one tolerates hour-long waits or robotic answers in a physical shop, they're not going to stand for it online.

Looking around, I don't find much evidence that business, large or small, sees what's coming down the pike. Too many organizations are still stuck in the brochure-ware era, when next-day or next-week response was acceptable.

So in this chapter we look at how you can engage people at the *precise moment* they are interested in what you offer.

Respond Now, While Buyers Are Hot

It's easy for a one-man or one-woman business to respond to inquiries in real time—especially in a recession. When things are slow you stare at the phone and check your email several times an hour. You leap on any opportunity as it comes in. But what happens when you're busy? And how do you cope if you run a global enterprise with thousands of employees?

The answer is automation.

By automation, I don't mean those stupid, impersonal, and frustrating auto-responders that "follow up" with canned email messages. The real-time Web response machine I'm talking about cleverly uses automation to help *humans* respond to inquiries as they come in.

If the successful outcome to each customer inquiry in your business involves a hefty price tag or significant revenue over the long term, you probably need this capability right now. If you sell business-to-business offerings you need this. If you sell cars or real estate you need this. If you seek parents willing to spend $100,000 or more to send their child to your college, you need this. If you seek generous donations to your charitable effort or political campaign, you need this.

You need this because the sooner you engage your customer's interest the more likely you are to win in the end. And today that interest frequently begins with an almost offhand Web search.

Someone mentions Kenyon College at a party so you Google it just to see if it might suit your daughter. Or you happen to see a photo of Madonna stepping out of a Maybach and wonder, "How much does a car like that cost, anyway?" If you engage people's first spark of interest you have an opportunity to fuel their curiosity and light their desire.

To learn more about Web-site response automation, I spoke with Mikel Chertudi, vice president of demand marketing at Omniture, an online marketing and Web analytics business unit of Adobe.

"When you contact people quickly, the propensity to close that business deal goes up astronomically," Chertudi told me. "Let's say you're interested in a new mobile phone. You might want a BlackBerry Curve or an iPhone, and you're looking for a local dealer. When you reach a web site you fill out a form that says, 'I'm interested, get back to me.' But if that company takes two or three days to respond, chances are that they're not going to reach you, because you're not in your office, or you're not at your house, or you already made the purchase somewhere else. But if they could follow up with you within five minutes, when you're still thinking about it, it's going to greatly increase the likelihood of a sale."

Chertudi says the automation process should collect two important pieces of information. Knowing the actual place on your site where the person expressed his or her interest allows you to reply in context. Similarly, it's important to know the nature of the offer that interested the potential buyer. If he or she downloaded a guide or an e-book, your salesperson needs to know that.

Armed with this information, the automation takes over. "An inquiry can send a real-time alert to a company salesperson, and the salesperson can just pick up the phone," Chertudi says. "You can have that sales lead automatically injected into a phone dialer. It can even contact the salesperson's mobile phone, then connect the Web-site visitor and the salesperson in real time. Or the system can pop up an email alert telling the salesperson what the visitor wants, so you immediately have a contextual basis for a conversation. All of that can be automated."

The key to this type of automation is that information coming in on the web site is tied, via an automated process, to internal systems for interacting with buyers. The links happen behind the scenes, alerting salespeople for real-time follow-up. In other words, the potential buyer's expression of interest triggers an action in the company's customer relationship management (CRM) and sales force automation (SFA) systems. The most important aspect is the trigger point—the point at which somebody actually raises his or her hand by filling out a contact form or responding to an offer. For example, anytime someone signs up for a Webinar, completes a survey, or downloads a research report, this action should trigger a response.

Chertudi says the best web site offers are ones that facilitate action. "When people with very busy schedules want to know, now, in the moment, the answer to a question, that's the best," he says. "When you know contextually what that person's intent is based on, what they're looking for on your site, and you're able to answer in real time, engage them further, create demand and accelerate the sales cycle."

Data from Omniture clients suggest that companies close more business when they address buyers' needs not in several days (which is typical) but within five minutes.

Know When She's Ready for You

A great example of real-time follow-up is Bella Pictures, a company that provides wedding photographers in 36 U.S. markets, including Los Angeles, San

Francisco, and Chicago. I asked Teresa Almaraz, channel marketing manager at Bella, how they manage to catch the wedding bouquet.

Bella partners with large wedding-information sites like The Knot and David's Bridal and uses search-engine marketing to attract buyers. Bella's own site features offers such as a contest to win a $4,800 wedding photo package and a free engagement photo session. One cool offer is the style tool that allows brides (yes, it's almost always brides; boys just don't grow up dreaming of weddings) to rate 20 pictures on such characteristics as indoor versus outdoor and posed versus candid.

"Brides love rating pictures," says Almaraz. "Then the tool reveals what kind of pictures are best [for them] with language like 'Oh, you're more of a romantic bride.'"

Whenever a bride-to-be uses one of the tools or responds to an offer, she's asked a series of registration questions. The answers are fed into Bella Pictures' automated systems. Almaraz says the company built a real-time lead-scoring system based on data mined from Salesforce.com (Bella Pictures' CRM system) and Eloqua (the company's marketing-automation system).

"The business modeler used statistics to tell us how likely someone is to set an appointment based on the different variables," she says. "We then take the data from each inquiry into Eloqua, which prioritizes the hottest leads for our sales team."

From a real-time response perspective, two questions are the most important indicators of urgency: (1) Do you have a wedding date? (2) Have you chosen a reception venue? When the answer to both is "yes," the system flags this inquiry for immediate follow-up, because positive answers indicate someone is ready to book a photographer *right now*. Weddings are about ritual—and rituals are highly predictable.

"Our leads are perishable," Almaraz says. "During the time people are actually purchasing photography services, they're sometimes meeting with five or six different photographers. So getting them on the phone right away is highly important for us."

The Eloqua system used by Bella Pictures funnels each inquiry, with the lead score, to the appropriate sales rep for follow-up. Each sales rep sees the information in an Eloqua dashboard. If the bride-to-be completed the rating tool, that information is displayed in the dashboard as well. "We provide information in a digestible way for sales to have the data at their fingertips when they need it to make the call. It's got their wedding date and venue. It's got their lead score. And we know what kind of photos they'd like, so the rep is able to contact the person immediately and say, for example, 'We noticed you're a romantic bride, and actually we have a great photographer we've worked with near you who shoots very romantic photos and would love to meet with you.' The more the rep knows about what brides are looking for when they respond, and the faster they respond, the more likely they develop a personal connection."

Test It Out!

For the automation process to generate the maximum volume of inquiries for real-time follow-up, you need to create and publish effective information offers or contact request forms.

Development of these offers and forms can itself be an exercise in real-time marketing and PR, because any offers you create can be tested in real time. Follow this procedure, which will allow you to choose the most successful offerings. So I recommend you create a number of offers, test them on your site, and then choose the ones that generate the best responses.

Chertudi says that Omniture frequently tests messaging and offers, measuring how successfully each one drives demand. "Every month, we produce three or four Webinars with experts, influencers in the industry," he says. "But before we put the final title on the Webinar, we test three to five different titles on a preliminary basis on our home page. And then, based on which one received the highest clicked response rate (meaning people fill out the form, download it, and give us their contact information), we'll use that as the title. We have found that the title of a Webinar has the most important influence in driving the best results."

What's the Other Guy Doing?

In a new field like this it's useful to watch the pioneers and benchmark your efforts against competitors.

Compete, a Web analytics and online competitive intelligence company, draws on a diverse sample of more than 2,000,000 Internet users' online behavior in search of insights for companies looking to improve their online marketing. These 2 million consumers have given permission for their online click stream to be analyzed as part of an aggregated population. In other words, each individual's viewing habits are not made available, but the aggregated data from the entire consumer panel is analyzed. "We see what 2 million people are doing, down to granular insights," says Stephen DiMarco, chief marketing officer of Compete. "Think of it as a cross-sectional view of consumers, instead of just looking at what is happening at your own site, which allows for competitive benchmarking analytics on which you can act immediately."

Compete's benchmarking analysis can be delivered into platforms (such as Omniture and Eloqua, mentioned earlier) used by sophisticated real-time Web marketers, enabling them to compare their performance to similar web sites. By understanding what's working on other people's sites you can often see how to improve your own. Here's one example that shows how.

Imagine you run a Chinese takeout restaurant with a Web-based ordering application. You can optimize your own site by testing for offers (e.g., if we put the main dishes first in the listing, do we increase the overall dollar amount of the average order?). But imagine laying on top of that data the collective information of how all Chinese takeout restaurants in the United States arrange their offers. Perhaps that data would lead you to an insight about featuring a "healthy option," something you had never even considered.

"A lot of marketers are now using A/B testing of multiple versions of content and tests for different offers, text, images or whatever," DiMarco says. "They use that to implement real-time marketing updates and landing page optimization." Adding the competitive benchmarking analysis component makes the A/B testing more valuable. "A major wireless carrier thought that they had optimized well using A/B testing," he says. "But we compared against other wireless carriers, similar industries, and the best of the Web and found something significant that they were not optimizing. We made a recommended switch, and that campaign won hands down. When you have a large site with lots of transactions—say, a mobile phone supplier—if a small tweak to the site generates a 1 or 2 percent increase that can be worth tens of millions of dollars."

The beauty of the external data supplied by Compete is that it provides a real-time benchmark of what's going on right now at sites similar to yours. So while your competitors are doing long-drawn-out focus groups or in-person surveys that take months to compile, you can be analyzing today's data *today*.

"It used to take a year to plan a marketing initiative," DiMarco says. "Now strategic marketing can be done on a weekly basis, and tactical marketing can be minute by minute. Marketing has an opportunity to move faster; it is the last holdout of efficiency in many organizations."

The more I learn about sophisticated tools like these, the more I look back at some of the crude tools we used to pretend were accurate metrics—and laugh.

15 Make the Sale

Having read this far, if you find all the changes we've covered a bit scary, I can't say I blame you. Just when you think you've got it figured out, here I am telling you that marketplace expectations are exponentially ratcheting up. Now, you're supposed to give each of a million customers personalized service in seconds. "Omigawd," you're thinking, "there goes lunch, forever!"

Stop and take a deep breath—because here comes the good news.

Highly sophisticated tools are emerging to help you stay ahead of the pack—if you have the real-time mind-set it takes to harness them effectively.

Your web site, as we discussed in Chapter 14, is the starting point. Online you need to match the best of bricks-and-mortar in every aspect, with service that is fast, responsive, personalized, friendly, customer focused, and brand consistent.

In this chapter we zoom out to consider other aspects of your corporate workflow. I want to show you how a focus on real-time data can transform your business in ways that drive sales performance.

Real-Time, Data-Driven Marketing and Sales

Have you ever heard a marketer try to explain what marketing is? "I'm in marketing," some dude tells his prospective grandmother-in-law. "I've heard of that," she responds, "but I've never been quite sure what it is, exactly. Is it like advertising?" Five minutes later he's still stammering on and she's wearing a puzzled expression.

Maybe this is why marketers and the agencies that support them spend so much effort and budget on clever creative. Normal people sometimes understand and even appreciate this aspect of their work. But all eyes are guaranteed to glaze over once they start talking about data analysis.

Sorry, grandma, from here on marketing will be increasingly data-driven. As the wired world ramps up the speed of business, marketing is going to focus on minute-by-minute gathering, analysis, and response to real-time data. Success is going to come from efficient internal data flow among marketing, sales, and senior management.

The future vice president of marketing is going to talk nonstop—and knowledgably—about CRM, SFA, analytics, and platform optimization. The big-picture and creative stuff won't disappear; he or she will still need to opine persuasively on the core legend of the brand, and such. But just like a bond trader talking to his clients, marketing execs in every field are going to look at the real-time numbers on their screens before every call to the CEO. Strategic discussions with the CEO will center on the trends these numbers reveal.

The key question is: What infrastructure is going to put what data on the screen they both consult?

> Business leaders adopting the real-time marketing and PR mind-set need to extend the model by building an infrastructure to enable real-time sales.

Now imagine the future business-to-business sales rep selling big-ticket offerings. In the new real-time, data-driven marketplace, what will his or her day involve?

It used to be these people would spend their time cold-calling from sales lists, or following up on leads from the most recent trade show. Already, prospects are more likely to pop up on the corporate web site in response to an offer than to appear at the trade show booth.

Assuming that ever more business migrates online, the key questions here become: What will the sales rep know about his prospective customer? What tools will help him or her respond in real time, based on an accurate understanding of the customer's needs and readiness to buy?

I won't keep you in suspense. Here is what the modern, real-time-enabled sales portal should look like:

As a buyer visits your web site and registers for a Webinar, an alert is triggered on the salesperson's real-time dashboard, providing details about the buyer based on the page that person is visiting. The alert notes that the person downloaded a white paper a few days ago. In fact, the alert is flagged as high priority because that combination of actions (white paper download plus webinar registration) is highly indicative of a propensity to buy. The alert automatically pulls up information on the buyer's company. Are they already a client? Have others from this company visited the site before? What do third-party information providers say about the company? News stories from Dow Jones or Bloomberg appear along with a company snapshot from an information supplier like Hoovers. Even the buyer's LinkedIn and Twitter profiles appear. And all this happens in real time.

Now this sales call is anything but cold. The sales rep initiates contact armed with up-to-the-second information. And that buyer is being contacted at the precise moment when he or she is most receptive.

Real-Time Technology

To support real-time business, you need technology infrastructure every bit as sophisticated as a financial trading floor. Let's take a look at each of the basic elements.

Technology backbone: A superhighway connecting all the computers in your company. Data flows through it at the speed of light.

Real-time news and commentary: Datafeeds from external sources including mainstream media, analysts, and information databases.

Real-time social Web: Real-time blog posts, tweets, online video, and other social networking content.

Real-time web site traffic: Information on your company's web sites updated in real time as people interact (see Chapter 14).

Customer database: Includes all existing customers and their purchasing history, plus records of who has contacted them, when, and about what.

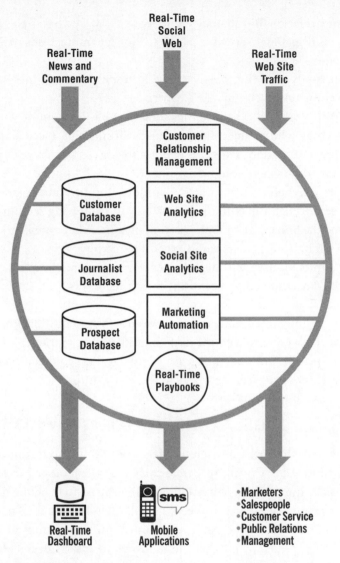

Real-Time Business

Journalist database: A database of known journalists and analysts, including bloggers and other citizen journalists (see Chapter 6).

Prospect database: Potential customers with information on how they found your company, which salesperson is in charge of the relationship, and status of discussions.

Customer relationship management: Your CRM system is the tool your sales and customer service reps use to manage interactions with existing customers and buyers.

Web site analytics: The tools you use to understand the interactions on your company's web site (see Chapter 14).

Social Web analytics: The analytics tools you use to monitor what people are saying on blogs and other social networking sites (see Chapter 8).

Marketing automation: The tools you use to engage with buyers, including email marketing and lead management.

Real-time playbooks: Best practice you develop in your organization to engage buyers for maximum growth (see the following section).

Real-time dashboard: The Web-based application that your marketers, PR professionals, salespeople, and executives use every day.

Mobile applications: Alert mechanisms delivering data from the portal via mobile devices to employees away from their desks.

When well integrated into an appropriate technology backbone these modules work together to feed the dashboard that your marketers, PR professionals, salespeople, and executives use every day. Let's look at several examples of how this overall scheme works in the real world.

I Heard You Just Came into Some Wealth!

This real-time dashboard approach to sales is not limited to business-to-business companies. Data-driven, real-time sales may be deployed in any enterprise. Consider nonprofit organizations and their need to generate donations.

I am an alumnus of Kenyon College, a small liberal-arts school in Gambier, Ohio. And I'm a loyal donor, each year contributing to alumni fund-raising campaigns. But it saddens me that the fund-raising efforts of my alma mater are stuck, like most colleges, somewhere in the 1950s. I receive fund-raising direct mail (dare I say "junk mail?") from Kenyon several times a year asking for money. About once a year, my dinner is interrupted by a well-meaning student volunteer on the phone who pesters me to cough up some cash. The only deviation from this pattern was in the lead-up to my recent 25th reunion when they redoubled their efforts.

Instead, imagine if Kenyon had real-time, data-driven technology infrastructure in place. If so, they would have known:

- From their own databases, that my daughter (with whom I share a mailing address) is now in high school, has visited the college, has participated in an admission interview, and is now on the admissions office mailing list.
- From their web site data, when I visited the site recently, I checked out the admission pages (unusual for me) and the swim team section. They know who I am because I registered on the site during a previous visit.
- From external data, that I've published several books in recent years and that I speak all over the world about marketing strategy. This would come up because my bio mentions Kenyon.

Now, imagine how the Kenyon College alumni solicitation *could* be conducted. The college might ask about my daughter: "Is she still interested in applying for admission? Oh, and by the way, would you care to donate today?" Or, how about if the college contacted me and said, "Congratulations on publishing your new book. We see that you'll be in Chicago on a speaking engagement in October. How about popping down to deliver a lecture to students and do a book signing? And by the way, how about stepping up your donation this year to the elite level, now that you're more successful?"

All this may sound a bit far-fetched to some people, but, in fact, all the tools needed for this level of real-time engagement are available today.

Once I started to consider how a nonprofit organization could do this, I looked around for solutions providers. And that path led to Shaun Sullivan, CTO of Blackbaud, a provider of software and services to nonprofits, including the University of Arizona Foundation, American Red Cross, Lincoln Center, and the WGBH Educational Foundation. Blackbaud supplies technology to support fund-raising, constituent relationship management, and web site management.

One Blackbaud application, ResearchPoint, delivers real-time data from public databases into a dashboard for fund-raisers at nonprofits.

"Say you're a major gifts officer and you've got a big meeting with the heir to a hotel fortune," Sullivan offers. "He's a major donor already, and you're about to ask him for $25 million. But you're notified on your mobile phone just before the meeting that he was just granted more company stock, or he executed some stock options at a certain value. Now you would know to adjust your proposal to ask for $40 million instead of $25 million. That's not the kind of thing you would have known if you did the usual: print your trip report notes out, hop on the plane, and do the meeting."

Blackbaud also uses information from nonprofit web sites to create scenarios for maximizing donations based on what people do on the site. The information on somebody who visits the site is added to the donor record in real time, and that may trigger a particular type of outreach.

"When the donor visits the web site and gives a credit-card gift over a certain amount, this automatically triggers some wealth scanning," Sullivan says. The system uses publicly available data (such as securities filings and property ownership) to identify the Web donor, and qualify them as a high-networth individual. "If that passes a certain level, the contact is routed to a prospect researcher." Then various scenarios for how to approach the donor are suggested to development officers. Perhaps a face-to-face meeting makes sense. "You know what the ideal communication path for a donor looks like. We follow that to get the best lift. That's powerful." And it was all triggered by a modest credit card donation.

Make Your Sales Team Love You

It's hard to find evidence of love between marketing and sales. At many companies the relationship is downright adversarial. Often, the tension extends all the way up to senior management. Like a marriage gone bad, the dialogue is an endless tape loop. Sales says, "Get me some good leads! These leads stink! My people can't sell." And marketing responds: "You got good leads! Your guys just stink at closing!" Having been in the middle of these "discussions" at several companies, I've heard it time and time again.

> Senior managers have a tremendous opportunity to lead the entire organization forward as a real-time sales and marketing machine.

Now, it's time for the lion to lie down with the lamb. New tools create the impetus for sales and marketing to pull in the same direction—if senior management shows the way!

Real-Time Sales Playbooks

Companies like IBM Software have used "sales playbooks" for years to reliably standardize sales processes that lead to successfully closing deals. These tools include all the information a sales rep needs to lead a buyer from initial contact through discovery and negotiation to close. Most include telephone scripts for contacting buyers at each step, prebuilt PowerPoint presentations, plus product data sheets and other collateral to deliver at each touch point in the process.

Sales playbooks are typically created by marketing, with input from the most successful salespeople on how they close a deal. The goal is to define a recognizable and repeatable selling situation. This is kind of like the checklist a pilot uses preflight, with each step identified in an easy-to-implement process.

For example, if an insurance company introduced a new product to cover vacation homes, the playbook might show the steps involved in contacting high-net-worth clients. It would make the process of selling the new product easily repeatable by hundreds of salespeople over thousands of customers.

Today's data-driven marketing and sales machines take this to a much higher level, providing sales teams with *real-time playbooks* that are powerful tools. This is particularly useful in outfits where marketing and sales are at odds, simply because implementing real-time playbooks focuses on a common goal: closing more business by optimizing for real-time marketing and sales agility.

"What we recognized is that salespeople very quickly become overwhelmed by too much irrelevant information," says Brian Zanghi, CEO of Kadient, a provider of automated real-time playbook applications used by large sales teams. "Too much information [delivered by salespeople to buyers] actually slows a deal down by forcing buyers to sift through what's important and what's not. We automate the playbook and embed a playbook application right inside the systems already used by companies. At each stage of the sales cycle, the playbook identifies the resources salespeople need in speaking to specific buyers in a variety of selling situations."

Resources might include a white paper, online video, or Webinar. The playbook prompts the salesperson in real time to engage with a buyer at each step and suggests what needs to be communicated and what information sent along. "With playbooks, it's also very easy for sales managers to make sure the company has done everything possible for salespeople to optimize their chance of closing every deal."

When playbooks are integrated into the real-time technology backbone, sales reps see the playbook information within the dashboard application they already use. The playbook includes full data on the product, buyer's contact information, record of previous contacts, and other details about the relationship right inside the dashboard the salesperson uses every day.

The playbook outlines the sales opportunity as a well-defined process through to closing. It outlines 5 or 10 basic selling steps in order, like verifying that the buyer can afford the product and has budget available, steps to counter-competing offerings in the middle of the sales cycle, and finally negotiating and closing the deal.

As no two sales are ever the same, you have to be ready to improvise when external events create a sudden opportunity—say, when once-in-a-century snow in Texas creates demand for your snowblowers.

If your sales and marketing machine is up and running at real-time speed, you should be able to create a new playbook on the fly.

"Imagine a sales team is selling to a particular marketplace and battling against a well-known competitor for new business," Zanghi hypothesizes. "If that competitor issues a press release to announce bad news—say, a product recall—in the old days it would have been impossible for a global sales team to identify the specific potential customers affected by that information, or to know when to contact them. Today, if a competitor makes an announcement that is pertinent to the selling cycle, it's very, very easy to modify that playbook. It's really easy to add a stage or an activity and for sales management to very quickly determine which opportunities, based on competition, sales must speak with now and within the next 24 hours."

With real-time sales playbooks, you can modify the script and roll it out instantly to each salesperson, so he or she can have a meaningful discussion with the contact. It is incredibly powerful for a rep to contact a buyer who is in the middle of a sales decision to say something like: "Hey, did you know the other company you're considering announced a recall 10 minutes ago?"

The examples so far are from larger organizations. But the same concepts apply equally well on a smaller scale. You need to monitor your web site traffic and reach out to buyers in real time. Using the free tools described in Chapter 8, you should monitor both mainstream and social media. And you ought to have existing and potential customers in your database so you can contact them quickly. Although the infrastructure in a smaller organization will be less sophisticated, what you can achieve is no less powerful.

Sales and marketing have moved beyond guesswork. Now is the time to implement a real-time sales and marketing machine at your company. Chances are that your competitors are not even thinking about these possibilities. When *you* bring marketing and sales together using real-time data delivery as the catalyst, your entire organization will be more efficient, your people will work together better, and you will drive more business to your company and away from your competitors.

They Know What I'm Doing!

When I talk about real-time, data-driven marketing and sales, people sometimes get uncomfortable. All this stuff sounds too much like "Big Brother is watching." People feel there is somehow a creepy, stalking quality to these ideas.

Sure, when I suggest that you monitor the news to see who gets stock options so you can hit them up for a charitable donation I can understand why that seems a bit predatory. That's exactly why it's imperative to use these tools sensitively.

To learn more about how people's behavior is used by companies in real time, and to get some of the privacy issues out into the open, I spoke with Brian Kardon, chief marketing officer at Eloqua, a marketing automation technology company.

"Not so long ago, a person might actually walk into a car showroom and ask a salesperson questions about the car they were considering," Kardon says. "Today, before walking into the showroom, a consumer has likely read multiple car model reviews online, posted status updates on Facebook and Twitter ['Looking at new Audi A4 . . . Waddaya think?'], downloaded product specs from Audi's web site, and a whole lot more. This is their digital body language."

There are hundreds of underlying consumer technologies that record digital body language that are embedded in the devices and services we use every day, including mobile phones, computers, credit cards, electronic toll collection, web sites, ATMs, Twitter, Facebook, LinkedIn, Google, and much more.

So, in reality, the only way to achieve true privacy is to live off the grid: No credit cards, no mobile phone, no Internet, no car, no bank account.

"Every day, consumers are leaving digital clues about their interests, intents, likes, and dislikes," Kardon says. "Like it or not, every move you make in the digital world is being recorded. That book you bought about vacations in Italy? Yep. That song you downloaded? Yep. That job posting in Philadelphia you looked at? Yep. It is all being recorded."

Companies like Eloqua extract data in real time and make it useful for marketers and salespeople. "There is a *lot* of data," Kardon says. "Eloqua processes more than 2 billion transactions a day. There is no way for mere humans to process it. And forget about Excel. You need huge servers to store the data, algorithms to analyze it, programs to segment it. At the core, marketing automation is about extracting patterns from huge amounts of data. In the most successful organizations, these three systems are integrated and provide one view of the world, processing your digital body language, and millions of others, often in real time."

As in any human interaction, discretion is essential in any contact with customers. So you will need to use what these new tools reveal about your customers with care and sensitivity. Doubtless, we're going to see some gaffes that make us wince. But I'm absolutely convinced that tomorrow's most successful marketers will be those who understand the new real-time technology infrastructure. The winners in the always-on world will be those who are most accurately and quickly driven by data.

16 Business at the Speed of Now

Congratulations, you've made it to the last chapter of this book! By this point, I hope you're convinced as I am of the real-time imperative facing business today. If you remain unconvinced, I hope at least you've found food for thought and some entertaining stories.

If you are convinced, though, you may face the dilemma I find that many people reach once they absorb these ideas. Where do I start?

I'll say it again: Business at the speed of now starts with a change of mind-set. Accept the challenge. Put real-time speed on your short list of top priorities. Rethink your assumptions.

I think this mind-set shift is much like the lifestyle change you make when you commit to a regular exercise routine. When I discuss the real-time mind-set, some people say "I'm too busy as it is, how can I add all this stuff to my day!" But that's what people say about exercise, too: They are too busy to exercise an hour a day. But once you build exercise into your routine, you don't know what you were doing before that was so important. Real time is the same.

Once you're focused on the challenge, implementing the changes you need to meet becomes straightforward.

In this chapter I offer you three diverse examples of real-time business at work. I relate how executives at General Motors embraced real-time engagement as the giant automaker emerged from the ashes of bankruptcy. Brian Halligan discusses how he created a software maker founded on real-time agility. Finally, you learn how musician Amanda Palmer turns disaster and delay into business opportunity on the fly.

The Mass-Media Aberration

In the twentieth century, business communication became a one-sided conversation: sellers talking at buyers through mass media. But it wasn't always that way.

In the premodern marketplace sellers and buyers related face to face in the bazaar. Vendors would make extravagant claims. Buyers would scoff and jeer in response. After a bit of haggling, both sides would agree on a price. If it turned out to be a rip-off, the vendor could expect to face angry customers next market day—and word of mouth would quickly spread.

From the mid-nineteenth century, though, newspapers and magazines began to assume an intermediary role between buyer and seller. As new media like radio and television appeared in the twentieth century, this intermediary role took on ever greater importance. Giant advertising and PR agencies arose to shape the conversation to suit the buyer, setting the agenda, the pace, and the tone.

Somewhere along the way, consumers lost their voices. They became an audience—listeners not speakers. So even when cheated outrageously it took huge efforts for consumers to voice their grievances. That's why United Airlines was able to assume they could ignore Dave Carroll's complaint about his broken guitar.

Nowhere was vendor/media power greater than in postwar Japan, where a handful of media conglomerates and a pair of giant ad agencies effectively dictated every word that reached 120 million unbelievably obedient consumers.

When I moved to Tokyo in the late 1980s, parking lots were filled with identical white Toyota Corollas. Prices stayed high because people believed everything was better in a prestigious department store's bag. Imports were rare because consumers were conditioned to believe foreign meant inferior. And young women were bizarrely content to let grouchy old men dictate their fashion choices.

The whole system began to unravel just as I arrived in Japan. As the yen doubled in value almost overnight and restrictions on overseas travel were lifted, young women flocked abroad in droves. Once they experienced shopping in Los Angeles, London, and Paris, there was no keeping them down on the farm. Japan Inc. quickly lost control of the fashion agenda.

The explosion of online communication has led to a similar loss of vendor control worldwide in recent years. With email, social media, and alternative online media, consumers suddenly regained their collective voice in the marketplace. Faced with a vendor's offer, consumers can once again scoff, rave, critique, or compare—and be heard far and wide.

All that canned laughter and applause you hear on television has been revealed as hollow, because now when someone runs a stinker ad on the Superbowl you can hear booing and jeering all across America in real time.

In Japan, meanwhile, young women tapping out messages on the subway now set a fashion agenda that veers all over the map so fast that dowdy department stores can't keep up.

Finally, we have a way to communicate like humans again. As in the premodern town marketplace, communication is once again real, personal, and authentic. Personal opinions matter.

Far from making everything "new," as many pundits insist, the Web has actually brought communication back full circle to where we were a century ago. What people respond to, and the way they make purchase decisions, really hasn't changed at all. The difference today is that word of mouth has regained its historic power.

The Web is just like a huge town square, with blogs, forums, and social networking sites like Twitter and Facebook serving as the pubs, private clubs, and community gathering places. People communicate online, meet new people, share ideas, and trade information. And yes, they sell products, too.

The twentieth-century mass-media era was a huge aberration in the history of communication. From the 1950s onward we spent six decades in a bizarre, one-sided, television-centered regime that gave no voice to consumers. But with the rise of the Web that era is over. We're breaking down the mass-media centered economy even faster than we built it.

In a real sense, we're going back to the way things were before the mass-media culture made us stop communicating in an authentic way.

> We need to unlearn what we've learned in the last half century about communication.

As this happens, mass media are not going to disappear. Media advertising will remain a key element in the marketing plans of any large business. The same goes for traditional PR and media relations.

Those traditional deliverables may still spark some useful discussions in your space. If you're lucky, when it finally appears (given the long lead times required for a traditional communications campaign) your message may still be relevant to the real-time discussion. It's more and more likely, though, that you will just arrive late to the party, with a message that sounds "so last week."

On-key or off-, relevant or not, it will no longer be enough to walk out on an expensive stage, blurt out your message, and return backstage. You must acquit yourself well in the discussion that follows.

Lutz and Me

Your message may be completely sincere. You may be actually walking what you talk. But for various reasons, fair or not, people are going to question your motives and call you on perceived contradictions. So you must be prepared to step forward and say, "Just a moment, here's proof that we mean what we say." Do that right, and you may be amazed by the results.

That just about describes the encounter General Motors and I had with each other.

If you want an example of "old-school" communication, it's hard to think of a better fit than General Motors. Over decades, GM invested massively in TV advertising and other traditional stuff like having Tiger Woods represent its Buick brand. What's more, after Michael Moore's 1989 documentary, *Roger and Me*—which featured hapless CEO Roger Smith ducking interviews—GM became a poster child for media nonengagement.

Having for years derided "The General" as a slow, clumsy giant, commentators lined up to kick the corpse when GM declared bankruptcy in June 2009. And I was among them.

As the bankruptcy was announced, GM launched what it called a "re: invention initiative" to assure the public (especially U.S. and Canadian taxpayers footing the bill) that it would emerge leaner and better prepared to succeed. This initiative included a web site, TV commercials, and full-page newspaper ads featuring a letter from president and CEO Fritz Henderson. The letter closed with this promise:

Over the coming days, months and years, we will prove ourselves by being more transparent, more accountable and, above all, more focused on you, our customer. I invite you to track our progress at GMreinvention.com. And on behalf of all the men and women doing the hard work of changing our company for the better, we look forward to showing you the New GM.

When I read this, I was extremely skeptical. What I saw was more of the same old marketing stuff GM had fed us over decades of decline: a cold, one-way, corporate approach that just feels inauthentic. Feeling a bit sad and depressed about this, I wrote a blog post under the title, "Attention GM: Here are the Top 5 Marketing Ideas for Your Reinvention."

In this snarky rant I questioned whether GM was really serious about reinventing the company's marketing and communications. I told GM, "Fire your Madison Avenue advertising agencies." All the expensive TV ads might make GM feel good about itself; all the golf sponsorships might get the execs front-row seats at Augusta . . . but none of that really engages with customers as GM promised.

Okay, so some of my suggestions were a bit vague: "Create products people want to buy." But one suggestion, "Humanize your company," caught blog readers' interest:

Sorry to have to tell you this: You are a nameless, faceless, corporation. Your ad in the newspaper today was signed by the CEO, but why no photo of him? Did he even read the letter that some marketer wrote on his behalf? The new TV commercial you launched today is an inane collection of stock photos together with a few cars. It is generic. With a few different cars, the ad could have been made by Chrysler. What about the people behind the reinvention? I want to meet the car designers. I want to know who the person is in your company who chose that weird color of purple of my latest GM rental car. People want to do business with people. Hey GM! Knock knock! Is anyone home? Who the hell are you???

Very quickly, many people commented on my blog and hundreds tweeted about the need to humanize GM. Emilio Bello wrote, "GM really needs to read this post!" Cal wrote, "Nice ideas. Will they listen? Probably not."

Andrew Rodgers wrote, "It really does look like the only way GM can make it now is to humanize the company, come down from the silver tower and listen to customers." And Robert Parrish wrote, "It's nearly impossible for dinosaurs of the 20th century to understand 21st century marketing." Many more comments expressed similar views.

To be honest, I assumed GM was so old school that no one at the company would even notice my post—much less respond.

Yes, We're Listening!

So imagine my surprise when I heard from GM soon after sending out my blog post. Christopher Barger, GM's director of social media, took time to engage during the busiest week in the company's history. He wrote, "With much respect, I'd offer that at least in the social realm, we are already doing much of what you're suggesting." Barger provided details and jumped in again to comment on my blog the next day.

You know what? Barger is right.

As I looked deeper into the swift re: invention process, I discovered that GM *is* beginning to humanize. It does engage in real-time communication. Wow!

One amazing, though characteristic, aspect of Barger's willingness to jump into the discussion on my blog was how the tone of the comments immediately shifted when my readers saw that a GM employee had commented. Rick Friesen wrote, "My thanks to Mr. Barger for his comment—I think this is a great response. I wish you all at GM the best of luck!" Elliot Ross wrote, "@Christopher: well done and good luck." John Cass even wrote, "David, this is a really grouchy post about GM. What have they done to you?"

Not all the comments posted after Barger's were positive. But there's no doubt that, simply by showing up, GM shifted the sentiment from universally negative to mixed, with many supporters. And all it took was a few minutes to write several sentences that tens of thousands of people read.

Several weeks later, on July 10, the day the "New GM" emerged from bankruptcy, in addition to the typical news conference for mainstream media, GM also engaged the public in real time on social media. This simple act served to humanize the company as I had suggested.

Not long after, Barger invited me to GM world headquarters in Detroit to meet top executives and ask what they are doing to humanize the company and engage buyers in real time.

When I got the invitation I was amazed that all this had stemmed from my snarky blog post kicking GM when it was down. I will freely admit: The real-time reaction, candor, and human interaction I got from Barger and his colleagues turned me from vocal critic to educated supporter. So I accepted the invitation and flew off to "Motown."

TweetDeck in Motown

When I sat down with Barger in Detroit, first thing I wanted to know was how he had noticed my blog post in a torrent of online chatter occasioned by the bankruptcy.

Barger told me that my post stood out because TweetDeck (the popular Twitter monitoring tool he uses) noticed that many retweets mentioning GM linked to my blog post.

"During the week we announced the Chapter 11 filing, everyone on the team here had TweetDeck going," Barger says. "Some people searched for mentions of 'Chevrolet' and others for 'General Motors,' or 'chapter 11.'"

When more than 100 people had tweeted about my GM blog post, referring both to the GM Twitter ID (@gmblogs) and mine (@dmscott), the Tweet-Deck searches Barger was monitoring made it easy to track me down. "It turned into a bit of a Twitter storm, so that's how we found you," he says.

Barger says he also uses an agency partner to help monitor the blogo-sphere. The agency provides data on trends, determines hot topics, and then provides the GM real-time team with a collection of representative or especially important blog posts.

Although Barger's real-time team includes only a handful of people, their work is catching on throughout the company. "What we have been trying to do, and what I enjoy seeing happen, is that the rest of the organization is now beginning to really pick up on the need to engage, the need to be aware of what's going on," he says. "It's great that people are beginning to recognize that these are valuable tools, that these are places where we can talk directly to consumers. That's very important."

GM Learns to Show Its Human Face

Since the momentum that took me to Detroit was generated by my offhand challenge to General Motors to humanize itself, that was the proposition I put to Mary Henige, who is in charge of both social media and broadcast communication at GM.

Henige responded by telling me how GM had always been part of her life. Both her father and husband worked for the company. She's been at GM herself for 23 years.

"It's easy to hate General Motors," Henige told me. "But people don't hate their Chevys. They love their Chevys. They love their Cadillacs. And the people who work on Chevys and Cadillacs, we love this company and the brands."

Henige says GM is now focused on letting employees, customers, suppliers, and other stakeholders tell their stories and the company's story on the Web. "You make it personal when you're able to tell a story," she says. "Now, through the power of YouTube and blogging, you're telling a story that seems very intimate. And you know when you've turned a consumer around, which is kind of thrilling. We still talk to reporters, and reporters are still very important to us. But you never quite know what is going to happen with the stories [written by reporters]. When you're telling your own story and you get that reaction directly from consumers, it's really important."

Lutz Always Gets the Last Word

If I needed further evidence that things are indeed changing at GM, just getting an audience with GM vice chairman Bob Lutz was proof enough. In the 1980s, even stalking poor Roger Smith didn't get Michael Moore more than a 30-second video clip. Twenty years later all I had to do was write a cranky blog post and—poof!—next thing I knew, I was on the executive floor, looking out at the Detroit skyline from high atop the Renaissance Center.

Bob Lutz is an outsize and outspoken character who will be remembered in the auto industry long after his retirement—at age 78!—in May 2010. Never one to mince words, the Swiss-born former U.S. Marine in 2008 termed global warming, "a total crock of shit."

Never short of opinions or shy about sharing them, Lutz began blogging way back in 2004. His FastLane blog paved the way for GM's social-media entry.

"For the CEO, or top leaders of the company, there's nothing more important than communicating," Lutz told me. "We are symbols of the brands and products we represent."

Once I raised the issue of social media, Lutz needed no more prodding. All I had to do was sit up straight and pay attention.

"One of the things about General Motors, and one of the reasons why we enjoy the antipathy of broad parts of the American public," Lutz said, "is they think we're all a bunch of stuffed shirts living in an ivory tower . . . that we don't care what people believe. We just do what General Motors wants. The more you can dispel that by engaging people, the more we can answer emails and get out blogs and get on Twitter and post stuff on YouTube, the more we make ourselves real, credible, and accessible and look like human beings who are trying to do a good job rather than a bunch of amorphous corporate types."

I'd just love to see Bob Lutz debate Michael Moore.

How Real-Time Communications Sells Cars

For GM, it's nice to have people like me think better of their company, but it's moving the metal that makes the bottom line. So how does GM plan to use the online world to drive bottom line?

GM executives told me that the most important influence on a customer's willingness to consider a brand or a specific model is the opinion of friends and family. Building that influence is their key goal in social media.

By harnessing the positive opinions of employees and satisfied customers, GM aims to "democratize" its message, leveraging the power of unbiased opinions coming from trusted sources.

So in the new GM marketing model, real-time word of mouth—what your family and friends say about a car, even online—is as critically important as it has always been. The back-to-the-future idea discussed in the beginning of this chapter, the idea that we've always communicated on a personal level, is clearly understood at GM. But the idea that people can also communicate online in a personal way adds an exciting new dimension to selling cars and trucks.

Now that huge investment in advertising is no longer a stand-alone. For GM, it is part of a comprehensive approach to drive awareness, generate interest, and drive people to the showroom, where they can actually make a purchase.

I watched GM put these ideas to work at the March 2010 South by Southwest (SXSW) festival in Austin, Texas. As a sponsor of the festival, GM offered visitors a chance to see the new Chevrolet Volt electric car—and even take a test drive. This aroused huge curiosity given the buzz around the advent of electric vehicles—and the fact that Chevy Volt is not yet on the market. People were shuttled to a nearby test track, where many got a turn behind the wheel. Since the Volt had not yet been heavily promoted in the market, the SXSW presence was a sort of coming out party for this revolutionary vehicle.

This opportunity to see and drive the Volt led to:

- 13,440 tweets.
- 1,216 blog posts.
- 1,268 other posts (including comments, photos, and videos).
- 33,500 page views through Facebook and ChevySXSW.com.
- More than 300 pieces of positive, user-generated content posted to ChevySXSW.com (including 250-plus videos).
- A 68 percent increase in the number of @Chevrolet Twitter followers in the month of SXSW.
- 8,764 new fans of the Chevrolet Facebook page.
- More than 250 mainstream media stories including *USA Today, AdAge, AdWeek, BrandWeek, Charlotte Observer, Detroit Free Press*, WXYZ-TV, and *Austin American-Statesman*.

"These are only short-term measurements of success," says GM's Barger. The ultimate goal in stimulating real-time conversation is getting people to drive to GM showrooms once the Volt is available. "The numbers are great. I'm thrilled with the initial results and increased visibility and connection for Chevrolet. But for SXSW to truly be considered a success, I'm looking months down the line."

Starting Up in Real Time

It takes huge effort to reset the clock of a humongous existing organization like GM to real-time speed. It's an altogether different challenge to get a start-up going at real-time speed from Day 1.

"The Internet fundamentally changes the time scales of business," says Brian Halligan, co-founder and CEO of HubSpot, an Internet marketing software company. (Halligan is my co-author on our book *Marketing Lessons from the Grateful Dead.*) "Because we started in the post-Internet age with people who live and breathe the Web, we run the business in a unique way. Instead of command and control, we empower people at the edges, and that changes the way you hire, promote, the hierarchy, and so on. We have a very different sense of trust and autonomy than most companies. And it has big importance for leadership."

Many companies tout their "open-door policies," but HubSpot has a "no door policy." There are no offices, even for the CEO. "It feels like there are fewer layers in the organization when anyone can just walk up to you with ideas. You can react to what's going on right away if you're not stuck behind a wall with a secretary guarding your door," Halligan says.

Since Halligan runs HubSpot as an always-on, real-time enterprise, the lines between "work" and "private time" blur to the point that the vacation policy was eliminated—people just take time off when they need it. "In my father's era, people worked 9-to-6 every day in an office," he says. "It was very structured, and he had to be in the office to get the work done. But our people have iPhones, and they are always online even on the weekends. It seemed very silly to us that people who sometimes worked for a few hours at home on a Sunday needed to formally request time off on a weekday. It just seems ludicrous to have this whole vacation policy so we said, 'Take whatever vacation you want; we trust you.' It's not command and control. Instead, it's very much about trusting and autonomy and pushing the decisions down so people can react in a real-time way."

The entire HubSpot organization is run on the Agile Scrum software development methodology. "The traditional way to develop software is called Waterfall," Halligan says. "That's where you develop very detailed product specifications and then you go away for a year to build off that spec. But what happens in business today is that in the year that you are building it, the requirements change quite a bit, so you deliver something that's just flat in the marketplace. Agile Scrum is the complete opposite. We never write detailed product specifications or plans. Instead we run monthly 'sprints' where we have four or five teams organized around a couple of developers, a product manager, and a designer, and they build to the product requirement backlog. When we make decisions on what to build, we change our minds like 10 times up to the very day before the sprint. It works extremely well because the competitive landscape changes in real time. As we get new input from customers, and we are able to react very, very quickly."

When Halligan told me about Agile Scrum software development I got excited. Here were the same principles I've been exploring in communication playing out in product development! Just as the traditional method of developing marketing programs takes tons of time, so also does the conventional method of software development. In both disciplines that added time means opportunities are missed.

Halligan says that working quickly is so essential to the HubSpot business that the Agile Scrum methodology has spread to other departments in the company. "Now marketing works the same way," he says. "So instead of a year-long marketing plan with all these lengthy campaigns, everything is on a monthly sprint cycle. We learn, we experiment as much as we can, and then we tweak it. We change our mind about what we are going to do a bunch of times between sprints, and then we typically lock it down the night before. The idea of working quickly is so essential to how we run our business."

The real-time management that Halligan has implemented at HubSpot is certainly paying off. "People want to work for an organization like this where they are empowered, where there is real-time decision making, and where things are not heavily planned in a command-and-control environment. So we have been able to attract very good people. We started three years ago with just two of us and now we have nearly 200 employees. We had no customers then and now we have almost 3,000 customers. We grew [by a factor of three] last year and we are forecasting a similar growth this year."

As I was finishing the manuscript to this book in June 2010, HubSpot was named by *Boston Business Journal* as the best company to work for in Boston (in the mid-sized company category). At the awards ceremony organizers said, "[HubSpot's] unique culture encourages innovative ideas in a fast-paced yet casual work environment . . . [that] fosters collaboration and integration between different team members. You'd be hard-pressed to find an unhappy employee."

Think about this! How can *you* move more quickly by empowering people to respond instantly to changes in the marketplace? You'll have happier employees, too!

Speaking of instant response, consider our next and final example. Your big revenue opportunity for the season goes up in smoke—more like ash, in this case—leaving you stranded in bizarre circumstances. Could you pull a rabbit from the hat faster than the rock star you're about to meet?

Improvising under the Volcano

Amanda Palmer, lead singer for the Dresden Dolls and punk rock cabaret solo artist, is active on Twitter (@amandapalmer has over a half million followers), her blog, Facebook, and MySpace. She uses Twitter as a tool for instant communication with her fans, frequently answering fans' tweeted questions and comments. "There's something about Twitter that's so different, because you're so accessible and it still kinda feels like a clubhouse," Palmer told me. "You're not just sending an anonymous transmission out to all of your fans ever who have signed your mailing list. Instead, it's almost like standing in a room with them and saying, 'Let's go over to this corner.'"

When she is on the road, Palmer uses Twitter and her blog to bring together groups of fans in real time. "I'll say, 'Last minute show at this bar. Everybody show up. It's free.' Or 'Here are the tickets; buy them now.'" She calls these instant performances "Ninja Gigs." Like the morning she tweeted word of a secret gig in Los Angeles: 350 folks showed up five hours later at a warehouse space where she played the piano.

Palmer has also done free Webcasts where she auctions off whatever she's got at hand: props from the videos she's just shot, handwritten song lyrics, even random stuff from her apartment, like an empty wine bottle. "People have bid hundreds of dollars on this stuff!" she laughs. "But a lot of it is not even really so much about the stuff itself as it is about their willingness to connect with me and support me," she says.

Palmer says that since early on in her music career, she's loved connecting directly with fans. "I've grown the fan base literally person by person," she says. "I've been saving money plus establishing huge connection with fans by 'twitchiking,' asking for rides to and from airports, etcetera, on Twitter. It works! But you must be fearless and have a fan base you trust. I also borrow practice keyboards from locals instead of renting for my hotel rooms, saving me almost $500 for every city I'm in. I've also been saving money on hotels, for example a $600-per-night hotel suite for a week in San Francisco for $150 by tweeting for suggestions and getting a tweet back from a fan who was a hotel manager. Fans *love* to help."

All of these ideas played out in real time for Palmer when she found herself in Reykjavík, Iceland, for what was supposed to be a 45-minute layover on an April 2010 journey from Boston to Glasgow where she was to perform.

That was the day Iceland's Eyjafjallajökull volcano erupted, shooting millions of tons of ash into the air and shutting down air traffic across the Atlantic and Europe. Palmer's flight was cancelled and her European plans were instantly erased.

Facing similar news, with a hotel voucher from the airline in hand, I think most people would just get on the bus and go sulk in the hotel. Not Amanda Palmer.

Instead, stuck in Reykjavík, Palmer got on Twitter—and got instant advice from people all over the world. "Hera Hjartardottir (@herasings), the Icelandic singer who'd just opened up for me in New Zealand, hooked me up with her childhood friend. And like magic I scored a ride from a stranger and didn't have to pack into the sardine bus to the hotel," she says. "We were friends within minutes." Palmer saw a few sights, had a refreshing soak in the Blue Lagoon (a natural geothermal spa), and ended up at the hotel in the early evening.

She then decided to do a Ninja Gig that night in Reykjavík. "An Icelandic comrade named Ben who had read my Twitter feed volunteered to find me a nightclub and equipment," she says. The gig was quickly confirmed, and Palmer tweeted the address of the bar and told people to get there at 9 P.M.

"We went and hung out on the streets of Reykjavík. I got a feel for the town and tried to encourage every lonely Icelander who was twittering 'am thinking about going to the @amandapalmer gig but it'll probably be too packed' that they were possibly the only six people that would be there," she says. "I played for about 2.5 hours, almost all requests. About 100 people came in the end. I drank six vodkas, and I did not pay for them. Afterward, behind the bar, I did an impromptu interview with Iceland's leading English-language paper while smoking a stolen cigarette, my first in months."

Can you believe this woman?! In the morning, she gets dumped at the airport of a strange city—Reykjavík, Iceland, of all places—by a bizarre natural disaster. How random and unexpected is that? Without missing a beat, by nighttime she's pulled off a gig that would take weeks of planning, even for locals.

It's about Focusing the Mind-Set on the Tools

Throughout this book—time and time again—I've told you, *It's about the mind-set*. And I've showed you—over and over—different ways people are applying that mind-set to the tools we now have at our disposal. They use mind-set and tools to successfully engage people in real time.

Amanda Palmer shows exactly how that mind-set functions when all the pieces of your carefully conceived plan get tossed randomly in the air. By nightfall, the real-time thinker has all the pieces reassembled in a completely different pattern. She's done it by reaching for the new tools she's mastered. In real time, she's engaged supporters, developed a local network on the fly, and crowdsourced creatively. And she got six free shots of vodka in the bargain.

Now it's your turn. May you have the wind at your back.

Appendix
2010 Fortune 100
Real-Time Speed Analysis

By Fortune *Rank*

Rank	Company	Response time
1	WalMart Stores	Did not respond
2	Exxon Mobil	unable to contact
3	Chevron	2 days
4	General Electric	3 hours
5	Bank of America Corp.	Did not respond
6	ConocoPhillips	Did not respond
7	AT&T	1 hour
8	Ford Motor	2 days
9	J.P. Morgan Chase & Co.	Did not respond
10	Hewlett-Packard	2 hours
11	Berkshire Hathaway	Did not respond
12	Citigroup	unable to contact
13	Verizon Communications	1 hour
14	McKesson	Did not respond
15	General Motors	unable to contact
16	American International Group	unable to contact
17	Cardinal Health	Did not respond
18	CVS Caremark	Did not respond
19	Wells Fargo	1 day
20	International Business Machines	Did not respond
21	UnitedHealth Group	Did not respond
22	Procter & Gamble	Did not respond
23	Kroger	unable to contact

24	AmerisourceBergen	Did not respond
25	Costco Wholesale	Did not respond
26	Valero Energy	Did not respond
27	Archer Daniels Midland	1 day
28	Boeing	3 hours
29	Home Depot	1 day
30	Target	Did not respond
31	WellPoint	1 day
32	Walgreens	Did not respond
33	Johnson & Johnson	Did not respond
34	State Farm Insurance Cos.	2 hours
35	Medco Health Solutions	Did not respond
36	Microsoft	1 hour
37	United Technologies	Did not respond
38	Dell	unable to contact
39	Goldman Sachs Group	unable to contact
40	Pfizer	Did not respond
41	Marathon Oil	2 hours
42	Lowe's	unable to contact
43	United Parcel Service	4 hours
44	Lockheed Martin	1 day
45	Best Buy	Did not respond
46	Dow Chemical	Did not respond
47	Supervalu	Did not respond
48	Sears Holdings	Did not respond
49	International Assets Holding	Did not respond
50	PepsiCo	Did not respond
51	MetLife	1 day
52	Safeway	Did not respond
53	Kraft Foods	2 weeks
54	Freddie Mac	Did not respond
55	Sysco	Did not respond
56	Apple	Did not respond
57	Walt Disney	Did not respond
58	Cisco Systems	Did not respond
59	Comcast	Did not respond
60	FedEx	Did not respond
61	Northrop Grumman	2 days
62	Intel	1 day

63	Aetna	Did not respond
64	New York Life Insurance	Did not respond
65	Prudential Financial	1 hour
66	Caterpillar	1 day
67	Sprint Nextel	1 day
68	Allstate	Did not respond
69	General Dynamics	Did not respond
70	Morgan Stanley	Did not respond
71	Liberty Mutual Insurance Group	Did not respond
72	Coca-Cola	1 day
73	Humana	Did not respond
74	Honeywell International	Did not respond
75	Abbott Laboratories	Did not respond
76	News Corp.	Did not respond
77	HCA	unable to contact
78	Sunoco	unable to contact
79	Hess	Did not respond
80	Ingram Micro	Did not respond
81	Fannie Mae	Did not respond
82	Time Warner	Did not respond
83	Johnson Controls	Did not respond
84	Delta Air Lines	Did not respond
85	Merck	Did not respond
86	DuPont	Did not respond
87	Tyson Foods	Did not respond
88	American Express	Did not respond
89	Rite Aid	Did not respond
90	TIAA-CREF	Did not respond
91	CHS	Did not respond
92	Enterprise GP Holdings	unable to contact
93	Massachusetts Mutual Life Insurance	Did not respond
94	Philip Morris International	3 days
95	Raytheon	1 hour
96	Express Scripts	Did not respond
97	Hartford Financial Services	Did not respond
98	Travelers Cos.	1 day
99	Publix Super Markets	2 hours
100	Amazon.com	Did not respond

2010 *Fortune* 100 Real-Time Speed Analysis in Alphabetical Order

Rank	Company	Response time
75	Abbott Laboratories	Did not respond
63	Aetna	Did not respond
68	Allstate	Did not respond
100	Amazon.com	Did not respond
88	American Express	Did not respond
16	American International Group	unable to contact
24	AmerisourceBergen	Did not respond
56	Apple	Did not respond
27	Archer Daniels Midland	1 day
7	AT&T	1 hour
5	Bank of America Corp.	Did not respond
11	Berkshire Hathaway	Did not respond
45	Best Buy	Did not respond
28	Boeing	3 hours
17	Cardinal Health	Did not respond
66	Caterpillar	1 day
3	Chevron	2 days
91	CHS	Did not respond
58	Cisco Systems	Did not respond
12	Citigroup	unable to contact
72	Coca-Cola	1 day
59	Comcast	Did not respond
6	ConocoPhillips	Did not respond
25	Costco Wholesale	Did not respond
18	CVS Caremark	Did not respond
38	Dell	unable to contact
84	Delta Air Lines	Did not respond
46	Dow Chemical	Did not respond
86	DuPont	Did not respond
92	Enterprise GP Holdings	unable to contact
96	Express Scripts	Did not respond
2	Exxon Mobil	unable to contact
81	Fannie Mae	Did not respond
60	FedEx	Did not respond
8	Ford Motor	2 days
54	Freddie Mac	Did not respond

69	General Dynamics	Did not respond
4	General Electric	3 hours
15	General Motors	unable to contact
39	Goldman Sachs Group	unable to contact
97	Hartford Financial Services	Did not respond
77	HCA	unable to contact
79	Hess	Did not respond
10	Hewlett-Packard	2 hours
29	Home Depot	1 day
74	Honeywell International	Did not respond
73	Humana	Did not respond
80	Ingram Micro	Did not respond
62	Intel	1 day
49	International Assets Holding	Did not respond
20	International Business Machines	Did not respond
9	J.P. Morgan Chase & Co.	Did not respond
33	Johnson & Johnson	Did not respond
83	Johnson Controls	Did not respond
53	Kraft Foods	2 weeks
23	Kroger	unable to contact
71	Liberty Mutual Insurance Group	Did not respond
44	Lockheed Martin	1 day
42	Lowe's	unable to contact
41	Marathon Oil	2 hours
93	Massachusetts Mutual Life Insurance	Did not respond
14	McKesson	Did not respond
35	Medco Health Solutions	Did not respond
85	Merck	Did not respond
51	MetLife	1 day
36	Microsoft	1 hour
70	Morgan Stanley	Did not respond
64	New York Life Insurance	Did not respond
76	News Corp.	Did not respond
61	Northrop Grumman	2 days
50	PepsiCo	Did not respond
40	Pfizer	Did not respond
94	Philip Morris International	3 days
22	Procter & Gamble	Did not respond
65	Prudential Financial	1 hour

99	Publix Super Markets	2 hours
95	Raytheon	1 hour
89	Rite Aid	Did not respond
52	Safeway	Did not respond
48	Sears Holdings	Did not respond
67	Sprint Nextel	1 day
34	State Farm Insurance Cos.	2 hours
78	Sunoco	unable to contact
47	Supervalu	Did not respond
55	Sysco	Did not respond
30	Target	Did not respond
90	TIAA-CREF	Did not respond
82	Time Warner	Did not respond
98	Travelers Cos.	1 day
87	Tyson Foods	Did not respond
43	United Parcel Service	4 hours
37	United Technologies	Did not respond
21	UnitedHealth Group	Did not respond
26	Valero Energy	Did not respond
13	Verizon Communications	1 hour
1	WalMart Stores	Did not respond
32	Walgreens	Did not respond
57	Walt Disney	Did not respond
31	WellPoint	1 day
19	Wells Fargo	1 day

Media Sources

Here are links to some of the articles, blog posts, and videos that are mentioned in the book.

Part One Revolution Time ────────────

Chapter 1 Grow Your Business Now

United Breaks Guitars Video 1
July 6, 2009
www.youtube.com/watch?v=5YGc4zOqozo

Taylor Guitars Responds to "United Breaks Guitars" Video
July 10, 2009
www.youtube.com/watch?v=n12WFZq2__0

Taylor Service, Air Travel Tips, and a Message from Bob Taylor
www.taylorguitars.com/news/NewsDetail.aspx?id=101

Air Guitar (Information on how to travel with a guitar)
www.taylorguitars.com/news/NewsDetail.aspx?id=99

Dave Carroll site
www.davecarrollmusic.com/

Calton Cases Dave Carroll Traveler's Edition Guitar Case
www.caltoncases.com/

Chapter 2 Speed versus Sloth: Dispatches from the Front

TMZ Breaks the News of Michael Jackson's Death
www.tmz.com/2009/06/25/michael-jackson-dies-death-dead-cardiac-
  arrest/

"Politico's Washington Coup" in *Vanity Fair*
www.vanityfair.com/politics/features/2009/08/wolff200908

Newspaper Death Watch Site
http://newspaperdeathwatch.com/

Google Finally Gets Real-Time
http://googleblog.blogspot.com/2009/12/relevance-meets-real-time-web
.html

Seth Godin Blog Post Announcing *What Matters Now*
http://sethgodin.typepad.com/seths_blog/2009/12/what-matters-now-get-
the-free-ebook.html

Chapter 5 Too Big to Succeed?

2010 *Fortune* 500 Full List
http://money.cnn.com/magazines/fortune/fortune500/2010/full_list/

Blog Post by John Winsor, Harry's Father, "Is Your Customer Service
Ready for the New World of Openness?"
www.johnwinsor.com/my_weblog/2010/04/is-your-customer-service-
ready-for-the-new-world-of-openness.html

Blog post: UPS Donates $1 Million to Haitian Relief—Here's How You
Can Help
http://blog.ups.com/2010/01/13/ups-donates-1-million-to-haitian-relief-%
e2%80%93-here%e2%80%99s-how-you-can-help/

Chapter 6 Engage the Media at Their Convenience

Kindle Community
www.amazon.com/tag/kindle/

New York Times "Amazon Erases Orwell Books from Kindle"
www.nytimes.com/2009/07/18/technology/companies/18amazon.html

National Political Do Not Contact Registry
http://stoppoliticalcalls.org/index.php

Zane Starkewolf for Congress site
www.zaneforcongress.com/

Rachel Maddow Talks about Zane Starkewolf Robocall (includes audio of the robocall message)
www.youtube.com/watch?v=hUg1C0VLQH4

Signal Integrity Blog
http://signal-integrity.tm.agilent.com/2010/signal-integrity-design/

GM FastLane Blog
http://fastlane.gmblogs.com/

Sacramento Kings Video Channel
http://tv.kingsconnect.com/

Chapter 8 What Are People Saying about You *This Instant?*

Blog Post: Who the hell ARE these people?
www.webinknow.com/2009/10/who-the-hell-are-these-people.html

Chapter 9 Tap the Crowd for Quick Action

BrandBowl 2010
http://brandbowl2010.com/

BrandBowl 2010 Results
www.mullen.com/2010/02/doritos-wins-the-brandbowl-budweiser-select-55-is-biggest-loser/

Crowdsourced Videos
HP—invent by Matt Robinson and Tom Wrigglesworth
http://vimeo.com/5437401

BrandFighters
www.brandfighters.com

Heineken Video Contest
www.youtube.com/view_play_list?p=7A05010CCB0AAAE3

DSB The Movie
In Dutch www.dsbthemovie.nl
In English www.dsbthemovie.com

Part Two Connect with Your Market ——————

Chapter 10 Real-Time Customer Connection

Justin Locke
www.justinlocke.com/

Montage Laguna Beach Resort
www.montagelagunabeach.com/

Montage Beverly Hills
www.montagebeverlyhills.com/

Rizzo Tees on the Web
Site www.RizzoTees.com
Twitter www.Twitter.com/RizzoTees
Facebook http://www.facebook.com/therealrizzotees
Blog http://rizzotees.posterous.com
Send eTshirts on Facebook http://apps.facebook.com/rizzo-tees-t-djhgih/
MySpace www.myspace.com/therealrizzotees
Blip http://blip.fm/rizzotees

Albion Cafe
www.albioncaff.co.uk/

Baker Tweet
www.bakertweet.com/

Cisco YouTube Videos
A Special Valentine's Day Gift . . . from Cisco! http://www.youtube.com/
   watch?v=3pffeMdDSoY
Happy Father's Day
http://www.youtube.com/watch?v=83jQVxaEII8

Domino Pizza Video
www.youtube.com/watch?v=OhBmWxQpedI

Maclaren USA Recalls to Repair Strollers Following Fingertip Amputations
www.cpsc.gov/cpscpub/prerel/prhtml10/10033.html

Running a Hospital Blog
www.runningahospital.blogspot.com

Baby Cory
Cory site www.singlebabies.com/

TippingPoint Labs
http://blog.tippingpointlabs.com/category/new-media-life-cycle-analysis/

Enter the Haggis
Blog brianhaggis.blogspot.com
Site www.enterthehaggis.com

Chapter 12 They Want It Immediately

Fair Disclosure Financial Network Awarded U.S. Patent for Innovative Transcription System
www.encyclopedia.com/doc/1G1-97307650.html

The Dead Books on Blurb
www.blurb.com/thedead
www.dead.net/features/interviews/jay-blakesberg-creates-magic-dead-tour-photo-books

Dead Tour iPhone app
www.jambase.com/Articles/17945/Dead-Tour-iPhone-App

Hollister Recruiting 2.0
www.hollisterstaff.com/recruiting2.0/

Pro Trading Course
www.protradingcourse.com/

Part Three Grow Your Business Now ————

Chapter 13 Let Them Communicate . . . Now

IBM Social Computing Guidelines
www.ibm.com/blogs/zz/en/guidelines.html

New Media and the Air Force
www.af.mil/shared/media/document/AFD-090406-036.pdf

The 3Rs of Social Media Engagement
www.exchange.telstra.com.au/training/flip.html

Telstra Launches Interactive 3Rs Social Media Learning Module
http://exchange.telstra.com.au/?p=896

Telstra's 3Rs of Social Media Engagement—Introductory Video
www.youtube.com/watch?v=XoWTZgq7q-I

Government of the United Kingdom Guidelines
http://coi.gov.uk/guidance.php?page=188

UK Government ICT Strategy
www.cabinetoffice.gov.uk/media/317444/ict_strategy4.pdf

Chapter 16 Business at the Speed of Now

My Original Blog Post
"Attention GM: Here are the top 5 marketing ideas for your reinvention"
www.webinknow.com/2009/06/attention-gm-here-are-the-top-5-
    marketing-ideas-for-your-reinvention.html
http://www.gmreinvention.com/

Video Interviews with GM Executives
Mary Henige, Director Broadcast TV and Social Media, www.webinknow
    .com/2009/09/mary-henige-of-general-motors-on-storytelling-and-
    humanizing-the-company.html
Christopher Barger, Director, Social Media, www.webinknow.com/2009/
    09/christopher-barger-on-social-media-communications-at-gm.html

Bob Lutz, GM vice chairman and the top marketing and communications executive in the company, www.webinknow.com/2009/09/top-gm-marketing-exec-bob-lutz-on-effective-communication.html

GM FastLane Blog
http://fastlane.gmblogs.com/

May the Best Car Win television commercial featuring Chairman Ed Whitacre
www.youtube.com/watch?v=jpqr4_ONew0

Information about the Corporate Culture at HubSpot
www.hubspot.com/culture/

HubSpot Named Best Company to Work For in Boston
www.hubspot.com/blog/bid/6082/Boston-Business-Journal-Names-HubSpot-the-1-Best-Place-to-Work

Acknowledgments

First, a disclosure: Because I do advisory work, run seminars, and do paid speaking gigs in the world that I write about, there are inevitable conflicts. I have friends in some of the organizations that I discuss in this book, as well as on my blog and on the speaking circuit, and I have run seminars or advised several of the companies mentioned in the book.

At John Wiley & Sons, my publisher Matt Holt and my editor Shannon Vargo have become friends as they have expertly guided this book and many others through to publication. Also at John Wiley & Sons, thanks to Kim Dayman, Deborah Schindlar, Peter Knapp, and Lori Sayde-Mehrtens for their help and support.

Kyle Matthew Oliver, Roger C. Parker, and Mark Levy read every word of each draft of this book, and their sound advice and practical suggestions made it much better. I'd especially like to thank John Harris, who helped me to see an alternative way to organize this book. Without John's input the book would have been far less interesting.

Dennis Daly at Dow Jones provided the data for some of the charts, and Doug Eymer designed them. Others who have been helpful include Nettie Hartsock, Michael Fix, David Henderson, and the members of JAF$C.

And especially, thank you to my wife Yukari and daughter Allison for supporting my work and understanding when I am under deadline or away from home speaking in some far-flung part of the world.

About the Author

David Meerman Scott's book *The New Rules of Marketing & PR* opened people's eyes to the new realities of marketing and public relations on the Web. Six months on the *BusinessWeek* bestseller list and published in more than 20 languages, *New Rules*, now in its second edition, is a modern business classic. David's popular blog and hundreds of speaking engagements around the world give him a singular perspective on how businesses are implementing new strategies to reach buyers.

For most of his career, David worked in the online news business. He was vice president of marketing at NewsEdge Corporation and held executive positions in an electronic information division of Knight-Ridder, at the time one of the world's largest newspaper companies. He's also held senior management positions at an e-commerce company, been a clerk on a Wall Street bond-trading desk, worked in sales at an economic consultancy, and acted in Japanese television commercials.

Today he spends his time evangelizing the new realities of marketing and PR by delivering keynote speeches to groups all over the world and teaching full-day workshops for companies, nonprofits, and government clients. His keynotes and seminars enlighten and inspire audiences through a combination of education, entertainment, and motivation. He has presented at hundreds of conferences and events in more than 20 countries on four continents.

A graduate of Kenyon College, David has lived in New York, Tokyo, Boston, and Hong Kong. He is on the advisory boards of HubSpot, Eloqua, Newstex, VisibleGains, Nashaquisset, the Massachusetts Air and Space Museum, HeadCount, and the Grateful Dead Archive.

Check out his blog at www.WebInkNow.com or follow him on Twitter @dmscott.

Have David Meerman Scott Speak at Your Next Event

David Meerman Scott is available for keynote presentations and full-day seminars. He is a frequent speaker at trade shows, conferences, and company events around the world.

David knows that sitting through a boring or off-topic speech is utterly painful. So he keeps things a bit edgy and uses stories and humor to make his points. But whenever he is in front of a group, be it 6 or 600, he provides valuable and actionable information about the new rules of marketing and PR, online thought leadership, and reaching buyers directly with Web content.

All of David's presentations are a combination of three things: education, entertainment, and motivation.

Visit www.DavidMeermanScott.com for more information.

Index